D1461603

A HEALING GUIDE
TO HAVING A BABY

Infertility, Emotional Wounds and Taking Back Your Power

JENNIFER COADY MURPHY

BALBOA.PRESS
A DIVISION OF HAY HOUSE

Balboa Press books may be ordered through booksellers or by contacting:

Balboa Press
A Division of Hay House
1663 Liberty Drive
Bloomington, IN 47403
www.balboapress.co.uk
UK TFN: 0800 0148647 (Toll Free inside the UK)
UK Local: (02) 0369 56325 (+44 20 3695 6325 from outside the UK)

Because of the dynamic nature of the Internet, any web addresses or
links contained in this book may have changed since publication and
may no longer be valid. The views expressed in this work are solely those
of the author and do not necessarily reflect the views of the publisher,
and the publisher hereby disclaims any responsibility for them.

The author of this book does not dispense medical advice or prescribe the use
of any technique as a form of treatment for physical, emotional, or medical
problems without the advice of a physician, either directly or indirectly. The
intent of the author is only to offer information of a general nature to help
you in your quest for emotional and spiritual well-being. In the event you use
any of the information in this book for yourself, which is your constitutional
right, the author and the publisher assume no responsibility for your actions.

Print information available on the last page.

ISBN: 978-1-9822-8540-1 (sc)
ISBN: 978-1-9822-8554-8 (hc)
ISBN: 978-1-9822-8541-8 (e)

Balboa Press rev. date: 07/27/2022

Dedication

To my fun loving husband Tom, fur-baby Belle, my loving parents John & Tina, dear family, friends & clients and all my incredible mentors who truly impacted my life and without whom this book would not have been possible. I thank you Bob Proctor, Hanne Marquardt, Eldon Trimingham, Stewart Blackburn, Anthony Larkin.

From my heart to yours, love, light and gratitude always.

Jennifer

Contents

Foreword

by Bob Proctor

I have been studying the inner workings of the mind for most of my adult life: Why we behave as we do and why we get the results we do. I've worked with clients and some of the largest companies in the world and have witnessed results that were previously unthinkable. Companies who sold more of their product in a month than they previously sold in a year. Clients who recover from an illness that was to have taken their life. Kids who were failing in school and end the year with As and Bs. First time mothers who were terrified to give birth, who delivered their baby with ease and calm.

The mind is the most intricate and complex computer system ever created, yet we're not given any user's manual or any assistance with how it works. Left to our own devices, we walk around blindly doing the same thing day in and day out and getting the same results, day in and day out. We wish for something better yet, many expect the opposite. Most people really want to do better. They even know how to do better and yet they don't. Why? Paradigms.

In today's vernacular, our paradigm is our operating system and controls everything we do – from the way we think, the grades we get in school to the amount of money we earn. Society too has its own paradigm, our way of doing things, what's expected.

Many people grow up with the idea that we grow up, get a job, find a life partner, and then start a family. But starting a family doesn't come easily to many people—even when they do everything doctors and modern medicine tell them to do.

So, what do you do when you desperately want to have a child, but no matter what you've done or tried, you haven't been able to conceive or carry a child to term?

You create a new paradigm!

Jennifer Coady Murphy has been where you are. After trying everything she could think of or afford to do to have a baby without success, she was overwhelmed with sadness and frustration. But then, she decided to take matters into her own hands.

In *A Healing Guide to Having a Baby*, you will discover a whole new approach to infertility as Jennifer takes you on a journey beyond the realm of medical science, blame, and excuses. She provides a system for getting to the root of your physical and mental symptoms and creating the right path for you—the one that can lead you to the healthy pregnancy you have been yearning for.

This inspirational and thought-provoking book will guide you through a challenging and introspective adventure of self-discovery to uncover, discover, acknowledge, and release your hidden emotional wounds and unresolved feelings that can lead to physical symptoms.

However, as powerful as the ideas in this book are, simply reading each page will not improve your chances of having a baby or changing *anything* in your life. You must do the exercises and act on the ideas to get the results you want. As you move through each chapter, you'll gain more and more insight into who you are, what's going on inside you, and what's possible for you.

Get ready for an exciting journey. If you think you can't have a baby because of your health, age, or financial status, this book can change what hasn't been possible up until now.

Bob Proctor, Best-selling Author of You Were Born Rich

Part 1
Infertility

Fertility Past

Beyond the Realm of Blame and Excuses

I know exactly where you are right now. The want, the need to have a baby is so overwhelming. Every thought is consumed by "baby, baby, baby." First thing in the morning, last thing at night, and about fifty thousand other times throughout the day. It is like a disease eating away at you. The mental turmoil, the ups, the downs, the highs, the lows. A roller coaster of hope and despair. Month after month. From "This is it; we're definitely getting pregnant this month" to "It's happening; I can feel it" to kicking yourself for kidding yourself into thinking you could be pregnant to "Oh, there's that pain I get every month just before my period starts" to hating your body for having a period. I can feel it all.

In this book, you will learn a whole new approach to infertility and discover why pregnancy has not happened as you had hoped for, yet. We will go beyond the physical symptoms, beyond the realm of blame and excuses to uncover, discover, acknowledge, and release your hidden emotional wounds and completely unblock your potential.

Visualise an iceberg, an enormous block of ice above the surface of the water. It seems insurmountable, impossible, and never-ending, like endometriosis, like multiple miscarriages, like unexplained infertility. But what is really going on, the actual problem, the even larger part of the iceberg, is underneath the surface. Emotional wounds—like fear, anger, frustration, abandonment, and betrayal—are the bigger issues, the ones underneath. If you can overcome the bigger part of the iceberg, then the top will melt away on its own.

Visualise the tip of the iceberg as your physical symptoms: endometriosis, multiple miscarriage, failed rounds of IVF, whatever you are experiencing right now. Now visualise the huge part under the surface as hidden, buried, supressed feelings, thoughts, things you wished you had said, things you wished you had not said, things you wished you had done, things you wished you had not done.

It is all this emotional stuff underneath that builds, festers, and creates those physical symptoms in the first place, so we must go deeper. Why do you have endometriosis? Where is it coming from? What is it connected to? What unresolved feelings have created endometriosis in the physical body in the first place? The same questions could be asked of miscarriage or any other explanations for infertility: Why is your body in fight-or-flight mode? Why doesn't your body feel safe enough to hold a pregnancy right now? What are the crippling fears, worries, and anxieties going on in the background? How does this all connect?

The goal of this healing book, my goal for you, is to help lift you out of the realm of blame and excuses so you can see the bigger picture and look forward to a bright future you can achieve and attain. Move beyond blaming yourself, blaming others, blaming circumstances, blaming past experiences.

Let's discover what is really going on in the background so you can experience and most importantly enjoy a safe, healthy, happy pregnancy.

We will go way beyond the stumbling blocks of blame regarding age, diet, or weight; they will not be mentioned in this book, but you will notice that they will also naturally and organically fall into place after going through this journey with me. You will heal emotional wounds that once drew you to comfort foods; as soon as those wounds are gone, you'll naturally be drawn to a healthier, more varied, and colourful diet.

You will notice wonderful changes in every aspect of your life. Things that used to really upset you will no longer make you flinch. Fears that once stopped you in your tracks and kept you from doing things or going places will dissolve. Upsetting work situations with colleagues will resolve and sort themselves out in ways you had not even thought of. Everything will change for the better.

You will release mindless labels, embedded commands, hurtful comments that doctors or others have made about diagnoses, age, weight, and so on. You will release the mindset that this whole "trying to get pregnant" business is out of your control or unknown or just one of those things. By discovering, acknowledging, and healing your emotional wounds, you will take back your power. Trust that these wounds will be gone forever, and you will be on your merry way to parenthood, loving your safe, healthy, happy pregnancy, and expanding your family.

Even better, you will enjoy the journey along the way. What is the point in being pregnant for nine months if you are going to be riddled with fears and worries? There is no fun in being afraid to bend down to pick something up, afraid to do things or go places, even afraid to use the restroom. My goal for you is that you not only become pregnant, but you enjoy your entire pregnancy and experience a safe, healthy, happy delivery at the end. Pregnancy is supposed to be an incredible, joyous time of radiance in your life. Trust you can experience it all: becoming pregnant, enjoying your pregnancy, and having a healthy delivery.

I know right now you feel exhausted, worn out, on an uphill battle. Let me reach my hand out to catch your hand; allow me to guide and inspire you forward.

Hear the words "I can, I will, and I am" echo in your mind. Allow them to vibrate and resonate throughout your whole being. Step by step, breath by breath: "I can, I will, and I am." One moment at a time: "I can. I will. I am." Get used to saying, "I am." Hear it reverberating as we continue.

Healing is always an individual and intimate process. You possess enough vitality for your desires, but you're often unable to access it when you need it, as it is stuck somewhere in your body, physically, mentally, or emotionally. By the time we have finished the journey of this book together, you will be standing tall on the top of a mountain, filled with vitality after climbing the tough terrain and overcoming the blocks and barriers along the way. Arms outstretched, feeling empowered, shouting out to the world, "I am confident, and I believe in myself."

I am so excited for you. You've got this. Remember: "I can. I will. I am."

My Personal Story

Excitedly, we decided to start a family and could not wait to be pregnant. We genuinely thought nothing of it and assumed we would get pregnant straight away, which didn't happen. After six months, we went to see our doctor, who told us not to worry, we were both healthy and well, and if nothing happens in the next few months, we'll run some tests.

Nothing happened, so we went back to the doctor, who arranged for us both to have tests. Unbeknownst to us, our own doctor went on early maternity leave before the tests returned. The doctor's office phoned and said we needed to make an appointment and come straight in for the results; something slight had showed up.

We had only sat down when the fill-in doctor blurted out nonchalantly, "You will never hold your own baby in your arms," and continued with all this medical jargon, terminology I had never heard before. I could not digest what she was saying; I had not even caught her name.

We were referred to a fertility clinic and had to go through all the tests again. This time, the results were not as bleak as we first thought, but that statement still echoed in the back of my mind: "You will never hold your own baby in your arms." Who would say such a thing?

During our IVF cycle, everything went like clockwork. We were a "textbook couple," they said. The clinic was not the friendliest place to be; you barely got a hello, and usually your bill was slapped up on the counter first. It felt like such a money racket, with so many hidden costs. We ended up paying double what we expected to.

You give all your trust to the professionals and are willing to pay anything for your dreams. The energy in the clinic was horrendous.

Couples sat in the waiting room, heads down. Nobody even spoke to each other. It felt like there was something in the staff drinking water; practically every nurse was pregnant, and they all seemed armoured with this defence that screamed, "Back off, lady; this baby is mine."

When it came to transfer day, talk about a Monday morning job: We had to be at the clinic, which was almost two hours away from our house, at seven in the morning. We were super excited. I had to have a full bladder beforehand for the scan. I was bursting to go by the time we arrived. We were brought into the theatre; my husband was placed in a chair in the corner behind me, and the extremely hungover-looking doctor came into the room. He looked sleep deprived, like he had been partying all weekend, which unnerved me instantly.

After I signed my name and date of birth on countless forms, the doctor proceeded to transfer the two embryos.

Another feeling of dread washed over me as the doctor looked around in disbelief and said, "It fell."

What fell? You dropped our baby on the floor? This can't be happening. He then proceeded to say, "I can't see it; it must have went in."

I was brought back to the waiting room and told to lie there with my legs up and not to use the bathroom for twenty minutes. By that point, I was so bursting to go—such pain, such fear. I was led to believe I would wee my babies out if I went. I waited and waited and waited. Thirty-five minutes later, I could not wait anymore; the pain was excruciating.

And after the intense two-week wait, the day finally came to do the test. I almost couldn't look.

Two pink lines. *Yay! We're pregnant!* Words cannot describe our excitement.

For those few weeks, it was magical. Every time I closed my eyes, I could see our babies in full detail. We were playing, singing, telling stories; it was like that was my time with them.

I stood frozen to the spot, like having an out-of-body experience. I had just overheard a young lady share the news with her best friend in the waiting room: "I'm pregnant; my life is ruined. I'm due Christmas Day." Only hours earlier, moments before my own first scan, we had been told we were due on Christmas Day. Our excitement was immense. Cold jelly on the belly followed by an eerie silence, and then ... "There's nothing there. The sac is empty."

As we drove from Cork to Waterford, I was crying so hard I couldn't see or barely catch my breath. I pulled myself together enough to go into work, where I could be distracted. For those few hours, I could pretend I was still pregnant, I wasn't ready to let that dream go.

My two biggest fears in life presented that day: fear of the past "being pregnant," fear of the present "not being pregnant": both right there, slapping me in the face.

Just one more massage to do before I could leave. After work, I sat in the car as a tsunami of tears rushed forward; I sobbed my heart out for over an hour before I could pull myself together enough to even start the car, let alone see the road through the tears.

Nothing could have prepared me for that day, nothing. We were so positive, so absolutely sure, that I had eliminated all doubt.

But now, "There's nothing there. The sac is empty." We were due Christmas Day. Ironically, my husband and I are big kids at heart and just love Christmas; it's our favourite time of year. The perfect time to have a baby.

"There's nothing there. The sac is empty." We were inconsolable. The nurse, obviously used to this situation, was not one bit empathetic; she said in the most monotone, empty voice, "You're going to have to get off the bed; other couples are waiting for their scan. Go to the hospital across the road for blood tests. Don't eat anything. It could be ectopic, which could be life threatening. You may have to have an emergency operation."

We were bombarded with all this serious information in the space of five minutes, with no time allotted for grief.

By contrast, the nurse who greeted us at the hospital was so kind, warm, and compassionate; she ran down the hall with the blood samples to get the results back quicker. Thankfully, I did not require an emergency operation, but the loss was just as devastating.

Until you have experienced a miscarriage, you truly have no idea the emotional ruin it causes. It is not just the loss of the pregnancy, but the loss of the whole life you had mapped out for your family, for you and your child.

After everything, memories of significant moments flooded back. Consciously, I was so focused and determined for the positive outcome we hoped for, but subconsciously, my attention and awareness had absorbed so much more.

Reflecting back, I can remember a lot of red flags. After the transfer, we were given free pregnancy tests, which instantly struck me as unusual because everything up until then had cost extra. I also had a Clearblue test on hand that determines how far along you are.

Out of pure curiosity, I wanted to see how accurate they actually were. Obviously going through IVF, everything is so scientific and measured. We knew exactly down to the minute how far along we were. But when I took the Clearblue test, "Not Pregnant" came up on the screen. *Wait, what?* I did the second test we were given from the clinic: two pink lines again.

Pregnant. Not pregnant. Pregnant.

When I rang the clinic with the results, they fobbed off the Clearblue result. Months later, I discovered the clinic purposely gave out the cheap tests that can react to the high levels of hormones you are pumping into your body throughout the process, frequently giving a false positive result. When we went back for a consultation, the clinic actually viewed that as a successful IVF cycle; when I mentioned the tests, they got defensive and blamed my going to the bathroom too soon after transfer as a possible reason for not being pregnant.

Throughout the procedure, we were made to feel old and incapable: "old eggs," "not enough sperm," "poor quality lining."

Lots of embedded commands to set the stage for blame should things not work out.

Yet we were hooked on their every word because we wanted it so badly and were willing to do whatever it takes. At the end of the day, it is a business, a sales process. Client after client are told the very same spiel, word for word. Just as a client who went through eight failed cycles of IVF said to me once: "You're brainwashed to believe you're infertile," that these kinds of options are your only hope; that particular client became pregnant naturally through the inner work in this book.

Please don't get me wrong. IVF is an incredible option for some people, but if you are stuck in a trap of failed cycle after failed cycle, or you are heading into each cycle consumed with fear, worry, and doubt, or perhaps even harsh embedded commands such as "You'll never hold your own baby in your arms" anchored in the psyche, it will not work. You have to go deeper; that stuff has to be cleared from your path first.

I discovered invaluable lessons on that journey.

Pregnancy is not just a physical thing; it is physical, mental, and emotional.

I'm here to enlighten you: Clinics are not your only hope. This process, this healing work, is your hope.

May you receive through this healing book the gift of reclaiming your own power, your self-trust, and confidence in your beautiful body, which is filled with innate wisdom, knowledge, and guidance.

May you experience your precious, deserved moment of holding your own baby in your arms; if anyone tells you otherwise, reject that information as untrue. Nothing is permanent, everything is changeable, everything is workable. You can overcome any challenge in this life.

Through turning to reiki, Kahuna healing, and reflexotherapy for my personal healing, I discovered the depth of my own healing abilities and capabilities. I am in the very blessed position of adoring what I do; it is a privilege and true honour to work so closely with couples on their journey to parenthood, to witness first-hand the overcoming of major traumas to watch them evolve and transform through inner healing, just as you will.

I am so grateful for my loving husband, our fur-baby Belle, our humble abode, and being able to clearly see that everything happens for a reason. I know that phrase might feel cliched right now, but I promise by the time we get through this healing journey together, you will find peace with it too, just as I did.

If we had not gone through that experience, I would not be doing what I am doing today. It brings me immense joy and happiness to guide couples through their personal journeys. Thank you for trusting me to guide you too.

> May you hear its gentle whispers as we move through this breathing exercise and beyond.
> Take in a nice, big breath, and exhale fully all the way out.
> For the next number of breaths, as you breathe in, in your mind, whisper the word "soooo."
> On the exhale, in your mind, whisper the word "hmmmm."
> Inhaling soooo.
> Exhaling hmmmm.
> See these words clearly in your mind, and elongate them.
> See all the ooooos, as many as you need to reach the soles of your feet.
> See all the mmmms rise up to the top of your head.
> Inhaling soooo all the way down to the soles of your feet.
> Exhaling hmmmm all the way up to the crown of your head.
> Begin to feel the powerful relaxing effects of these words.
> Powerful words with a powerful message of safety and deep relaxation.

Continue on for several rounds.

Inhaling soooo, all the way down to the soles of your feet.

Exhaling hmmmm, all the way up to the top of your head.

Continue this pattern as you feel your body responding with each and every breath.

Just breathing in.

Just breathing out.

Feel your body relaxing.

Feel your muscles releasing.

Feel your tension and tightness softening and melting away.

Now that we are relaxed, I want to give you one final word of encouragement.

We all experience challenges, pain, grief, loss, and turmoil in our lives. That may sound daunting, but you are not alone in this, and you can overcome any challenge life presents to you. Remember, you would not be here if you had not survived everything else to date. You've got this; together, we will work through the barriers impeding you on your journey to parenthood.

You know, deep down, this is going to be the breakthrough when everything changes, when you finally manifest your deepest desires. This is the sign you have been waiting for. In a simple yet powerful way, you know it and can feel it.

You've spent so much time playing small, caught up with the words of your inner critic, listening to others, feeling like you were not good enough, keeping yourself busy, overcomplicating your life to avoid listening to your intuition, to avoid facing the truth about who you truly are. You deserve to be a parent.

You feel the urge to take your power back and reconnect with your true nature. Deep down, you know you are meant for so much more. You know you have the potential to be creative and make a real difference in this world. Being a parent makes it even more important to you. Your intuition is telling you all of this is possible. But you don't know how. You're about to. I will guide you and show you the way.

I promise you, this is going to be so different from what you've heard before. You will be transformed.

May you have an abundance of courage, confidence, and self-belief in your inner power. May you achieve the positive success you desire and are truly worthy of receiving.

Love, light, and aloha
Jennifer

Now I have a random question to ask you, so the very first vision, image, or impression that pops in, please work with that.

❖ Bring your awareness right down to your womb.
❖ If you were to see your womb as a room, what does it look like? What is the very first image, vision, or impression that pops in?
❖ Is it light or dark?
❖ Is it small or big?
❖ Is it cluttered or clear?
❖ It may seem dark at first, so just allow the light to flood in; turn on the lights or imagine windows if you need to in your vision. If the room seems too big or too small, begin to adjust the size so it feels right. If the room is cluttered, begin to clear it out.
❖ If anything feels out of place in the room, take it out or transform it to something else.
❖ Now, stand in the centre of the room; what does it feel like?
❖ Begin to alter the feeling, making it feel warm, welcoming, and inviting. Fill this space with joy, happiness, gratitude,

fun family togetherness, open communication, acceptance, connection, abundance, whatever feelings you need here.

❖ Now, find the perfect place in your womb for your baby to nestle into, to be held, loved, and adored. Nurtured and cared for. You can even place a little light here, so your baby knows exactly where to go.

❖ Now, stand at the doorway; to the right and to the left, there are corridors or hallways.

❖ Look down to the right; is it long or short? Light or dark?

❖ Begin to shorten it if it's too long and add in light if it's too dark.

❖ Is it cluttered or clear? Are there things swept under the carpet? Begin to clear this space as your intuition guides you.

❖ Now step into this space; what does it feel like? Change the sensations so it feels warm, welcoming, and inviting.

❖ Walk down along the corridor or hallway; at the end, there is a door. Reach your hand out, open the door, and look inside; can you see your eggs, or are they hiding?

❖ If they are hiding, that's okay; bend down as if you were going to greet a toddler and beckon them forward. Give each and every egg a great big hug, and thank them for being your amazing eggs. Tell them how grateful you are to see them and how much you trust them; watch them transform before your eyes.

❖ What do they look like?

❖ Ask them what fears, worries, and concerns they have; listen to their answers, no matter how silly or random they sound. Give them this opportunity to be listened to and heard. Give them the reassurance they need to settle those fears; watch how they respond to your guidance and see how they transform to being healthy, bouncy, vibrant, ready, willing, and eager. They are your eggs for a reason; they have this incredible wisdom within and know how to join with your partner's sperm and fuse together to form an embryo. They just needed to be acknowledged and trusted.

❖ Now, gather up all your eggs; walk them down along the corridor on a little field trip or dress rehearsal. No matter which egg is released, they all know exactly where to go and what to do.

❖ Show them the beautiful room you've created and the perfect place you've chosen for your baby to nestle into to be held, nurtured, loved, and adored.

❖ Notice there is no competition at all here; they are all super supportive of each other.

❖ Explain the process of how they are going to meet a sperm, fuse together, multiply and divide, form into a zygote and into an embryo and nestle into the lining of your womb.

❖ Check in again in case any lingering fears, worries, or concerns pop up; settle any fears. Your intuition will guide you; trust it.

❖ Clearly see an image of your partner's sperm; what do they look like? Check in and ask them if they have any fears, worries, or concerns; do they need any assistance at all to transform into vibrant, healthy sperm with great motility?

❖ Follow your intuitive guidance; see your eggs and his sperm as magnetised, drawn to each other. Visualise the moment of conception clearly in your mind, and feel the power of that moment in your heart.

❖ Now thank your eggs and your partner's sperm; do a big American touchdown, "yay, team" effort. Thank them again, and guide your eggs back to their space; check in on their space and see if any adjustments are needed. Make any changes necessary.

❖ Look down to the left side; what does that side look like? It's a different side, so it may be a completely different experience. Is it long or short? Light or dark? Cluttered or clear? What does it feel like?

❖ Make all the changes necessary; add in or take out as much as you need to create a wonderful welcoming space. Walk down along the corridor, open the door, and check in on your eggs.

❖ Can you see them, or are they hiding?

❖ Beckon them to come forward; give each and every egg a great big hug.

❖ Thank them for being your beautiful eggs; ask them what fears, worries, or concerns they have. Listen to your eggs, regardless of what surfaces.

❖ Guide them down to your womb and show them the perfect place you have chosen for your baby to nestle into. Explain the process so there is no confusion; no matter what egg is released, they all know exactly where to go and what to do.

❖ What does that feel like? Reassuring? Empowering?

Physical Ailments and Fertility Past

Now we will look at physical ailments in a whole new way, with a whole new concept that even the doctors do not know about, although such physical ailments (endometriosis, cysts, low sperm count, fibroids, miscarriages, etc.) are very real physical experiences in your body.

Physical ailments always have an emotional tie or shadow in the background, creating a frozen effect beneath the surface, keeping things stuck and stagnant, feeding a repetitive cycle of pain and frustration. These emotional ties are like icebergs; they build and fester under the surface, building, forming, and actually creating your physical ailments in the first place. It is not just one of those things that you are experiencing this physical ailment, pain, or discomfort.

Visualise an iceberg clearly in your mind; see the enormous top of the iceberg, undissolved matter pushed up and floating on the surface, waving a red flag, wanting to be acknowledged. See it as your manifested physical symptoms floating on the surface, craving your attention, but what's underneath is actually the biggest part of the issue. Know that if you overcome the biggest part of the iceberg underneath the surface, then the top just melts away. All the unresolved emotional issues, hidden under the layers, have created your painful situation. The part on the top that you can see, it looks enormous, like endometriosis, like this astronomical stumbling block, but what's underneath is much bigger. Miraculous changes occur in every aspect of your life when this hidden area is acknowledged, released, and healed.

If you're trying to conceive, and all this emotional stuff is tucked away, hidden, building, and festering beneath the surface, stuck in your body, stuck in your womb, each and every disappointment and heartache along the way only adds to it. It's time now to connect the dots and allow a deeper understanding to unfold.

Fertility Past: Breakthrough

If only becoming pregnant was simple, and the truth is, it is, kind of. Perhaps you even believed it would be simple and thought to yourself, *I would like a baby*, and hey presto, that would be it, instant pregnancy that month. In an ideal world, that is what would happen. But it does not work out that way. Possibly you thought it was going to take a while, but that time frame has passed also. I am sure you are thinking right now, *If it was simple or easy, I would be pregnant by now.*

Maybe you are feeling frustrated, irritated, sad, or upset; please know, that is actually a really good thing. Fertility is a topic people often dread or fear discussing; strong emotions are triggered. If any emotions surfaced at all, it shows you that you really do want a child in your life, but something in your subconscious mind is blocking it. This book describes powerful techniques which can guide you directly to that block. You will learn how to acknowledge that blocker, identify where it resides in your physical body, and release it.

What usually happens is, you psych yourself out. You doubt yourself and begin to lose confidence and trust in your body and in your capabilities. You ditch your positivity and decide to stop; you get bored or frustrated doing all the things you know you should do and enjoy because you are stressing about doing them perfectly. You're questioning, controlling, and second-guessing everything. You are trying everything possible and still end up thinking, *It's never going to happen*. You're frustrated and let everyone else's ideas and opinions filter in. You google your symptoms and diagnose yourself with bleak negativity.

Before you know it, you are in a spiralling state of anxiousness and confusion, procrastinating like crazy, which only adds to the stress. Maybe you have developed a procrastination habit, an obsession with timing, day of the month, apps on your phone, or social media. Maybe you are fed up with yourself or hate your body for failing you and letting you down. Yet you are still ready to finally achieve your goal, like a never-ending emotional rollercoaster ride.

Does that sound about right? I see you. I hear you. I know that icky feeling you get in your belly when things don't work out as you planned, asking, "What's wrong with me? Why can't I have a baby? Maybe I am not cut out to be a mother; I am not worthy. What if my baby hates me?" It is so frustrating; wanting a baby brings up so much stuff, all your inner fears. But it has nothing to do with desirability or deservedness; you are just as deserving as anyone else in the world. In fact, why not you?

So if you are serious about understanding and changing the underlying emotional blocks impeding you, then you are in the right place. Despite all the doing, all the trying, and all the desire in the world, you might just be missing a crucial piece in your mindset. I am here for you. My mission in life is to guide you to your own inner healing and harness your inner power for your fertility journey. May this be a wonderful adventure where you grow, learn, and overcome.

Without any trace of blame or excuses, just understanding with kindness and compassion. Trust my guidance. In some way, you are holding yourself back, ignoring some inner guidance that you perhaps think is totally unrelated, which makes things harder. You might be wondering, *Why? Why would I do that?* It is actually really common. Nobody has thought that having a baby is allowed to be easy; society, family beliefs, or social media often denote struggle, sacrifice, hardship, loss.

My philosophy has always been, a safe, healthy, happy pregnancy is available and accessible. I believe this challenge you are experiencing right now is possibly the most amazing opportunity for inner growth and releasing the past you will ever experience. It will bring you to this blessed place of freedom, liberation, and joy. Just because it has not happened yet, it does not mean that it will never happen. It just means that something needs healing, something must be let go of, beforehand.

When you look at this situation in a whole new perspective, everything changes. This is the most amazing opportunity to pave the way for abundance in your life, abundance of joy and happiness. It's the opportunity to create the freedom to actually experience lots of family fun times without the shadowing, sabotaging fear of turning out like your mother or father, or whatever else is currently lingering in the corners of your mind. I believe pregnancy should be a radiant, joyous experience, and it can absolutely be so, but that is not what the world teaches us. We live in a culture where pain, suffering, and stress are almost expected, where parenthood is supposed to be hard. It is not socially acceptable to make it look so easy or fun, exciting, or enjoyable, especially now, when so many people are suffering. Ease and simplicity are almost frowned upon.

Retraining your subconscious to release those sneaky beliefs will be a total game changer. It is something you can learn, and it's the actual missing piece between people who struggle for years and people who are able to conceive naturally and easily. It is normal to feel sceptical or think that this stuff will not work for you, but know that it will.

My role is helping you in a very specific way. For the last decade, I have worked with thousands of clients, helping them transform their mindset with an incredibly practical system that works to stop the old sabotaging patterns of behaviour. This guiding work has helped thousands of people across the world in all aspects of their life. Even though clients may have only sought help for one issue in their life, the positive ripple effect resulted throughout all areas. Their entire relationship with themselves and those around them completely changed. They reported massive changes: rekindled romances, better relationships with family and friends, a more joyous and rewarding work life. Their eating habits changed organically; they became lighter, brighter, healthier, and happier. Now it is your turn. This is your time to thrive.

I will share with you three important ways your mindset is holding you back. You might be aware of some of them, but you may discover some new nuances you did not consider before. Trust me on this: The difference between frustration and a safe, healthy, happy pregnancy is mindset, and not in an airy-fairy way, like "just relax" or "be positive."

There are some really practical things you can do to train your brain for positive success. Change your thoughts, and change your word. Pregnancy is not just a physical affair; it is physical, mental, and emotional.

The physicality of pregnancy itself is pretty simple; it just takes one egg and one sperm, but without dealing with and understanding the underlying sabotaging emotions and behaviours, any pregnancy advancements will be rejected by your body, in a way of protecting you. This results in a cycle of numerous failed rounds of IVF. Your body listens to your fears and wants to protect you from them. Until you know what those fears are, it is always going to feel hard, and your efforts will be met with pain and struggle. You should know that you can decide today to step out of your own way and limiting beliefs, but how do you actually do that?

If you hear the word *mindset* and think, *Oh, no, I have to meditate every day or only think positive thoughts,* rest assured that you don't. That is only looking at it from a surface perspective; what I have learned from guiding thousands of clients is that we have to come at it from a deeper perspective or multiple angles. Visualise an iceberg; those fears and blocks are sneaky, hidden beneath the surface. They will find your weakness, and those old sabotages will pop up when you least expect them, when you are feeling low, or when you are about to do something big and exciting, like finding confidence, taking back your power, trusting and believing in yourself.

So to dig a little deeper and come at fertility from different angles, we are going to break it up into three parts: your fertility past, your fertility present, and your fertility future. I am going to give you some questions to think about, and I have a special request: I ask that you invite them in and let them percolate.

I am going to trigger you a little. As you ponder these next questions, new layers will reveal themselves to you. So please be kind to yourself. Allow whatever is ready to come up and surface. Neither wilfully create nor suppress any images, visions, or impressions. Just simply allow them to arise, and give yourself permission to acknowledge them. Veils will be lifted, and new layers will reveal themselves to you. The key here is to find out your inexplicably linked behaviours and patterns. Once these are acknowledged, it's like a child on a swing in the playground who yells out, "Look at me." Have you ever noticed that? All they want is acknowledgement; your fears are the very same. You do not need to delve into anything.

Your awareness, along with permission to release, is enough to free you, so you can move forward on your journey. You will receive answers about your fears, negative behaviour, and procrastination around fertility. Things like "Why can't I get pregnant? Why am I overanalysing and stressing out about pregnancy? Why don't I feel worthy?" You will be able to connect things from your past to your present, in a way you never thought possible.

You will be able to connect old beliefs and circumstances from your past to your present in unimaginable ways, and in turn, you will be able to create a new fertile future with the positive results you desire. Not by magic, but by design, through this powerful mindset shift. I have never worked with someone I could not help in some way. Thousands of success stories, people from all backgrounds, income levels, all around the world. The difference between struggling and finally feeling ready and worthy are your inner thoughts and beliefs.

Regardless of where you are starting from, how far down your path of trying everything, or no matter how long you have been on this journey, you can break free of the old limiting beliefs that are currently running in your subconscious mind, right now.

You may have tried several different options; the problem in hopping from "trying this" to "trying that" is, you take your subconscious beliefs with you. Unless the inner work is done, the outer reality cannot change. This work will tip the odds in your favour. If you change your thoughts and your inner beliefs, you will change your world, regardless of what any doctor's prognosis told you previously.

So let us begin at the start, your past; before we do, let's just pause for another moment together and take in a big, big, deep breath all the way in and exhale fully all the way out. Just to ground ourselves. We can take the time; you are worth it. For the next number of breaths, as you breathe in, add in those powerful words, inhaling sooooo, exhaling hmmm. In your mind, just whisper the word soooo on the inhale, draw your breath all the way down to the soles of your feet. Exhale hmmmm all the way up to the top of your head.

This breathwork is the fastest way of counterbalancing stress, worry, and tension. If you think about it, when you are stressed, worried, and anxious, your breath is predominantly caught in your chest, usually with short, rapid breaths, barely reaching the diaphragm, let alone going beyond; where is your womb, above or below the diaphragm? You need your breath to reach and nourish your womb and the whole reproductive system, so it knows that it is vital and important. Otherwise, it will not work to its optimum level and will even shut down completely due to high levels of stress and anxiety.

So come into a nice, open place now, feeling grounded, safe, and secure. You're open to receiving, learning, and discovering. Now, connecting to your past, go way back. Everything that happened to you, conscious or not, has contributed to how you relate to pregnancy right now. Your memories and beliefs from the past fundamentally shape how you think and feel today. Whether they are from your upbringing, your parents, your ancestry, or even ex-partners, these memories can create trauma and stories that hold you back from becoming pregnant and receiving a child into your life.

One of the keys of changing your future is to understand and heal from those experiences. None of them define you, and together, we can write a new legacy. Previously in most generations and cultures, usually only men were able to hold economic power. That means that most women in your lineage have been at the mercy of male-dominated systems: the church, the government, and the head of the household. Many women who did not get married were encouraged to either become teachers or serve in the church, where they took a vow of poverty, a vow not to marry, a vow of abstinence, and a vow not to have children.

Those subconscious patterns repeat themselves over generations. Some families have a feast-or-famine experience; one generation has lots of children, sixteen and counting, the next generation has none, very few, or plenty of struggle having children, while other families have one traumatic event that has repercussions for centuries, like a child sadly passing, disabilities, abandonment, abortion, or adoption, all having significant unbeknownst effects.

Even if you do not know your family's history, you probably have a sense of the last couple of generations. Chances are that your great-grandmother was not able to vote, hold land, get a mortgage, or even have a bank account, yet she was expected to raise eight to sixteen children. Your grandmother may not have worked at all, and your mother may have had to leave or give up her job when she married or had a baby. In your generation, there may not be any role models to look up to when it comes to balancing: having a career and having a family.

Having both could still be a taboo in your subconscious mind. Maybe you have not acclimatised to what that would look like. It might feel unsafe. It might feel unethical, stressful, hard work, exhausting. It might even feel like you are not quite ready, which is totally understandable.

There may have been a lot of secrecy around pregnancy or a scandal in your family. So please be kind to yourself, and have some compassion for your past, as it could be new territory to have it all: a job you adore, a family you love, and the enjoyment of being a mum. It is scary to be the pioneer; it might even bring up feelings of guilt or shame. Why should you have it all, when generations before you suffered, and people in the world are still suffering today? It may not seem fair, but the only people who are really bothered by that are people who would actually be the most incredible parents and make the world a better place, people like you: truly caring, thoughtful, kind, compassionate, worthy, and deserving.

Most of us grew up in a society where having a baby is a huge sacrifice; it's restrictive. So even though having a baby today is theoretically easier, we have far more help and resources, but that is not what we believe inside. It is challenging to compute and hard to wrap your head around the fact that anyone, even you, especially you, can have it all: joy, happiness, career, family, travel, when perhaps your own parents could not. You may have grown up witnessing your parents struggle, juggling to pay bills, and feeling a sense of sacrifice. You may even feel guilty about putting pressure on your parents. Let's be totally honest; is there a part of you that kind of resists pregnancy on some level?

23

Let us journey together now and spend time working through your early childhood memories, really mining for experiences that altered your beliefs in that fundamental way. What was your first experience of pregnancy? Who was the first person you remember being pregnant? How was that pregnancy perceived? Was it a joyous experience, a traumatic experience, or was it gossip central: a scandalous pregnancy out of wedlock? Maybe your mother was pregnant with your sibling; perhaps their arrival impacted you by taking your parents' attention away. Maybe you had to take on more responsibility around the house and help look after younger siblings, which left a lasting negative mark. Allow yourself to remember the impact; was it upsetting? You will be surprised how deep these layers can go, but know that healing from anything is possible. Especially now that you have the right support. Thinking about what I said so far, what do you think is your story of your fertility lineage?

Every family has an official or unofficial belief that family members either live by or rebel against; some feel oppressed by it. Invite this family belief to surface now; let it resonate within, and bring your awareness to it. Invite any images, visions, or impressions of your upbringing to come forth. You might even see an image of a family crest and values represented by this crest. Whatever it is, no matter how random it may appear, trust it; it is surfacing for a reason. These inner, inherited, absorbed beliefs are kind of sneaky. You may never have put two and two together, but now something is triggering. The bell of your awareness is ringing.

These beliefs and mottos get passed on and expressed through habits and behaviours. They get passed down in fears, worries, and concerns about who can and cannot become pregnant; maybe it's a taboo in your family to have a child out of wedlock or in a same-sex relationship. There may even be beliefs of how many children you can have and by when; thirties or forties maybe too late, according to your family values. So your true capabilities might be capped right now because you are living by these invisible beliefs and unofficial mottos. Even if it was true and right for your family up until now, it does not have to be your experience. We live in a completely different time now, where the circumstances of your birth, upbringing, gender, sexuality, physical ability, faith, ethnicity, appearance, or age do not dictate your ability to have a baby.

That is not denying the reality of the world; discrimination and inequality still exist in places today, but remember you are allowing this to be a reality for you, tipping the odds in your favour by doing this essential inner work. The very thing you can control in this situation is how you think and what you choose to believe. Energy flows where attention goes. But first, you must identify what it is that you are actually thinking and where your attention is (usually on the very thing that you do not want). You must give yourself permission to prosper and shine, regardless of what other people think. Your infertility past does not have to dictate your fertility future. But you must acknowledge it before you can heal from it.

Identify what your family beliefs are around pregnancy. It does not have to be anything elaborate. It could just be a couple of words, like sacrifice, hard work, difficult, or maybe words like resilient or proud, denoting struggle in a roundabout way. It could be a phrase you've heard repeated your whole life, such as "There's no easy way to have a baby" or "You'll have nothing with children," basically your family version of "Money doesn't grow on trees," whatever baby-related or pregnancy-equivalent phrase you grew up listening to.

For example, I grew up hearing "You were my smallest baby and my biggest ouch," said through gritted teeth and a pain-stricken facial expression; I too felt the pain each and every time I heard it. I even developed a phobia against pregnancy; for a long time, I could not even look at a pregnant lady, but never connected the two. Another phrase I heard over and over growing up was "It's nice to be important, but it's more important to be nice." The women in my family sacrificed and struggled; they did not have it all, but they were really nice, respected ladies. I had to acknowledge and change those beliefs that pregnancy and birth caused great pain, sacrifice, and suffering. That is simply not true.

25

Like the law of attraction, what you send out, you get back. What you think about, you bring about. Energy flows where attention goes. Those embedded commands are hidden beneath the surface, but after you acknowledge them for the sabotaging fears they are, you know that fears are really only thoughts, and thoughts can be changed; they soon feel like nonsense. I say nonsense, not to discredit anything you've experienced but to purposely speak to your subconscious mind, giving it permission to change and delete this old belief that no longer serves you well.

We change our minds all the time about things: what we are going to eat, what we are going to wear, or where we are going to go. When broken down, fears are just thoughts (usually untrue thoughts that will never happen anyway), and thoughts can be changed. Rest assured, by the end of this book, you will be empowered to notice if and when they arise. We are creatures of habit, and you might trip up sometimes, and that is okay. You are now developing the power, tools, and skills to acknowledge your thoughts and change them instantly.

If your family does not value creativity, you might unconsciously sabotage all aspects of creativity; giving birth to new ideas, change in general, may be challenging for you, not to mention pregnancy and giving birth physically. Did you know that your creative energy resides in the womb, along with your emotions? They may be subconsciously blocked, hence blocked tubes.

Even positive family values may impede you on your journey, something like "We never quit," or "We are so proud of our roots," so if you are stuck in something, you may feel you have to keep slogging away at it, the only way you know how; one subconscious reason perhaps why couples get trapped in continuous cycles of failed round after failed round after failed round of IVF. I have encountered couples trapped in this harrowing pattern; on some subconscious level, changing tactics would be disrespectful to the struggle of their ancestors, caught in this trap up to sixteen failed rounds of IVF. We are all shaped by our family legacies, whether we know it or not, whether we believe it or not. But it is empowering to know you can free yourself from the grasp of the past and shape your future.

So what do you do about it? First, never underestimate the power of awareness. When you are aware of these patterns, you can stop unconsciously living by them, rebelling against them, or being oppressed by them. You can consciously choose a different path. Then you can seek out other examples and surround yourself with more positive people so you can truly believe that it's also possible for you.

Begin to join the dots in your awareness, connecting between your past experiences, phrases you grew up listening to, and terms you heard over and over, the struggles you observed others enduring when you were a child.

Recap

Recall to mind the circumstances of the first pregnancy you were ever aware of:

> Was it a positive or negative experience?
> What was your first memory of pregnancy in general?
> Was there a great loss and devastation?
> Was there a scandal or gossip around the pregnancy?

Did someone fall pregnant out of wedlock or at a shameful age (too young or too old)?

For now, just simply allow these memories to surface, invite these questions to percolate and filter in. Neither willfully create nor suppress any vision, image, or physical sensation. When a memory arises, please notice where you feel it in your body.

What does it feel like?

Now put an image to it; what does it look like? Go with the first thing that pops in, regardless of how random it may seem. How can you change the image? Your subconscious or intuition will guide

27

you; trust it. For example, if you experience a knotted sensation in your stomach, and it looks like a rope, that image can be changed and released by unknotting it, delicately untying it like a knot in a necklace, or maybe it needs to be cut away altogether.

Trust that your intuition will guide you to do exactly what it needs to be freed.

Now change the image that surfaced for you, and experience the profound effects and change in your body.

If several scenarios surfaced, find where each one is anchored in your body. Think of each phrase or situation individually, one at a time, and observe where you feel it in your body. What does it feel like? Put an image to it; change the image, and feel the physical change in your body. No need to delve into anything; no need to worry or analyze, just simply acknowledge. Like that child shouting from the swing in the playground, "Look at me," they just need acknowledging. We all need to be acknowledged and listened to. Your body is the very same.

This is your time. You are ready for this healing step. I am here for you. I believe in you. You've got this.

I can. I will. I am.

Unexplained Infertility

The mighty call you feel to parenthood is there for a reason. Because it hasn't happened yet, it does not mean it won't happen at all; it just means that there's something within you that needs to be acknowledged, healed, or released first. That's all.

Did you know that you carry your emotions in your body? Physical ailments in the reproduction system are really cries for help. Your body is carrying and holding onto so much suppressed feeling, fears, and emotions that are in the way; it is asking you, "What do you want me to do with all these emotions?" It is begging you to address them, so it knows you are ready to let them go before it can do what it was designed to do.

While you should accept diagnoses of physical ailments and medical conditions, I urge you not to develop a fixation on the prognosis. Everything is changeable. I know this pain is very real for you; I'm not suggesting you don't actually *have* these medical conditions. I'm saying you can heal what's caused them in the first place, and by doing so, you can heal the medical condition completely. These diagnoses are offering you the chance to change, to improve, to heal, to grow. You've been given this enormous opportunity to look inward, to bring your attention to removing your own blocks and truly transforming your life; you'll finally understand on a deeper level what all this means for you in your life, and you'll have the added bonus of never having to fear these conditions reoccurring in the future.

If you have unexplained infertility and nothing has worked so far (you're eating the right foods, exercising, meditating, doing yoga, acupuncture, IVF, IUI, and so on), know that unexplained infertility *is* explainable, from a holistic approach. You have to look deeper to find the hidden cause of your ailment, the emotional wound or limiting belief in the background. Doctors tell you they can't find a medical reason why you're not pregnant, but something is blocking your fertility. Hidden wounds, beliefs, fears, anger, jealousy, resentment, anchored remarks, comments, and even trauma can block your way. Your body shuts itself down to keep itself safe in the midst of these kinds of deep issues, and it cannot function properly until they are uncovered and healed. Your mind believes those emotions, and your body heeds your mind, so it does not feel safe to conceive or carry a pregnancy to full term.

In this case, nothing else you're doing can work. You must heal the hidden beliefs and emotional wounds in the background for you to feel empowered and truly be ready, as opposed to thinking you are ready. Later in this book, we'll discuss how these issues prevent your body from becoming pregnant or being able to hold a healthy pregnancy: abandonment, abuse, adoption, abortion, bitterness, betrayal, and bereavement. Perhaps you experienced a devastating loss of a child or have a child with an illness or disability; you may fear there's something wrong with your next child. Maybe you still carry wounds from your parents' divorce or from betrayal by a partner or friend. Maybe you are afraid, afraid you won't be a good enough mom, afraid you'll end up like your own mom, afraid of the birth process.

These deep-rooted issues keep you from getting pregnant. Most of them unknowingly linger in the corners of your mind, creating havoc in your body. I'm here to guide you safely to and through those issues, some of which you may not even know are there. This is my expertise. Trying to bypass these fears and going straight to IVF or any other treatment method will not work. Even after years of struggling, people have gotten pregnant naturally through this work, and you can too.

Sarah and her husband went through eleven rounds of IVF. They remortgaged their home three times to pay for the treatments. Sarah, who was adopted, unknowingly had deep-rooted emotional wounds from her own adoption and feared she would not bond with her child the way she thought her birth mother couldn't bond with her. Once those fears were acknowledged and released, Sarah was pregnant naturally within one month. They have a beautiful daughter now.

This is just one of hundreds of examples I could give of what is possible in your life. As soon as you discover your emotional wounds and acknowledge them, it's like flicking on a light switch; it may sound outrageous, but you can conceive instantly. Have you ever seen a child run up to a mother, saying, "Mom, Mom, Mom, Mom," trying to get her attention, and as soon as the mom acknowledges the vocal barrage by saying, "Yes, love," the child just runs off? This healing work is the very same. Like the child in this example, your wounds don't need anything other than acknowledgement and reassurance. Your body needs reassuring. You need to believe and trust in your body that it can conceive. And that starts with healing.

How much do you trust your body right now?

If you have little to no trust and feel as though your body is letting you down, how can you expect it to produce this beautiful, healthy baby you're longing for?

You need to wholeheartedly create a safe environment of trust and happiness in your body, especially in your womb, and feel that safety and trust throughout your pregnancy, throughout all the transitions your pregnancy will bring, and extend that safety and trust into your parenting abilities as well. Yes, there will be challenges along the way, but nothing you can't handle or overcome. It's critical to shift from a place of stuckness, feeling as though your life is on hold, to allowing everything to flow and fall into place.

Allow your mind to be at peace. Give yourself full permission to trust in yourself and believe in the process of life. Your body knows how to get pregnant; it's already preprogrammed with innate wisdom. Your eggs are eggs for a reason. They're not kidneys; they're eggs. They know how to conceive and grow into a zygote, multiply and divide into an embryo. They just need the opportunity to be trusted to do so.

Secretly feeling guilty, being afraid you won't enjoy motherhood, or fearing you'll miss out on career opportunities also has a huge impact, creating mistrust within yourself, on some level developing an impression that you have to sacrifice one over the other, that you're not allowed to enjoy both. Know that you can enjoy both. Only then can your body feel safe in your decision to get pregnant.

Go deep within; discover how your body is affected by stress. Negative self-talk affects your neurochemistry, which affects you physically. If you think hopeless thoughts (*I can't get pregnant. I've tried everything. It's never going to work*, etc.), your body will respond to those devastating thoughts by tensing, tightening, and shutting down. If you think and feel positively (starting with "What if I *could* get pregnant?" to "Maybe I can" to "I know I can. I will. I am."), your body will happily respond by opening up, finally making pregnancy possible.

If you are on this journey to parenthood with a partner, you must both be in alignment. The woman who's trying to become pregnant often carries all the responsibility on her shoulders, feeling like she's the one doing all the work, going to all the varied appointments, eating the right foods, making sacrifices, giving up alcohol and coffee, and so on. It's a total game changer when your partner takes as much interest as you and steps onto this path with you side by side, both of you going forward, hand in hand, reaching your shared goals together.

Right now, if you feel hopeless, lost, frustrated, let down, angry, bitter, or confused, then your womb looks more like one of those crammed houses from a hoarder's program on TV than a peaceful space in which to grow a baby. This may sound completely overwhelming, but keep breathing. There are no limits. We'll work together to clear out that emotional clutter in your womb and create the beautiful, warm, welcoming, safe, nurturing space you need for your baby to come into. Not only that, but physical miracles will happen; cysts will disappear, fibroids will go away, endometriosis will vanish, tubes will unblock, babies will be conceived, and safe, healthy, happy pregnancies and deliveries will be experienced.

Do you feel like a failure as a woman for not being able to conceive? That stops now. You're strong. You're beautiful. You're powerful. I'm not giving up on you, so don't give up on yourself. I believe in you. My wish for you is that you believe in yourself, that you know your inner power, strength, and capabilities.

> Allow the words "I can, I will, and I am" to resonate in your mind.
> I can.

I will.

And I am.

Recall to mind the image of someone or something that brings an instant smile to your face, someone who sparks joy in your heart just by bringing them to mind.

Smile. Breathe in. Breathe out.

Feel your smile spread across your face. Feel joy overflow from your heart.

Hold onto your beautiful, unique smile.

Hold onto the joy and gratitude in your heart.

Gather up that positivity in your mind, and lift your head high.

You are empowered.

I can, I will, and I am.

Four As of Infertility

Abandonment, Abuse, Adoption, Abortion

The four As of infertility are abandonment, abuse, adoption, and abortion; these situations manifest as deeply anchored emotional wounds, preventing pregnancy. We will delve deep into the subconscious mind to discover, uncover, acknowledge, and release your deep-rooted emotional wounds, blocking your potential.

Abandonment

For those who are unaware of them, emotional wounds of abandonment are a huge stumbling block on the road to parenthood. Deep-rooted, unresolved feelings of abandonment form like brambles and thorns in the seat of your psyche, manifesting in physical ailments such as endometriosis or cystic masses on the ovaries or fallopian tubes. You may feel frightened, afraid to get too close for fear of being left behind; instead, you harbour strong feelings of unworthiness and insecurity.

This internalised fear of utter abandonment and loneliness stems back to your childhood; it creates toxic, heavy feelings of shame in the subconscious mind. You feel, "I'm not important," or "I'm not good enough." Everyone else's needs are more important than yours. You fear being your true self, hiding how you feel and who you are, putting on a facade in order to be accepted out of fear of being rejected. But that inner pain stays with you, becoming a harmful driving force in your adult life.

You hide the feeling that your accomplishments are never acknowledged anyway; they're always discounted; this is one of the underlying issues of miscarriage, the other being timing, feeling on some inner level that the timing is off.

Abandonment plays detrimental havoc until it is acknowledged. When doing visualisation work in the womb, dark images of thick, dense bramble bushes, long pointy thorns branching out in all directions, or images of being backed into a corner always surface, which need to be cut away. If something is beginning to surface, know that you are okay. No need to delve into anything; simply acknowledge where those feelings are being felt in your body. What does it feel like?

Now put an image on that sensation; what does it look like? Use your intuition as guidance; remember, you have all the tools in the world in your imagination, so whatever helps the subconscious mind to cut through or change the image, it is right there at your disposal. Clear the path, change the darkness to light, make the space bigger if it's too small, see a helping hand reaching out to draw you forward. Begin to create an inviting, warm, welcoming space, a home of acceptance for yourself and your baby, a home of connectedness for you both. You are important. You are worthy.

Karen suffered excruciating endometriosis, painful heavy irregular periods, blocked fallopian tubes, fibroids, and ovarian cysts for as long as she could remember. After years of struggle and trying everything, she found this self-empowering work. I was her last hope; she and her partner had been through seven failed rounds of IVF. Karen was angry, bitter, and in constant pain; she never smiled, often snapped, and was always on edge. Behind all of that, there was a heart of gold waiting to be healed, a truly kind generous person. During this work, anger and rage towards her parents surfaced, which surprised her; she had "come to terms with everything" years ago.

After going deeper within, Karen felt betrayed by her father when "he upped and left one day"; she was seven at the time. She always felt as though she was stuck in the middle, going between her parents, but she never expressed how she truly felt, as she didn't want to upset her parents, especially her mother; she was upset enough already. Karen suffered immense constant pain. Pain was written all over her face; her body was tight and tense. She was on so much pain medication, she had irregular, excruciating periods. She lived with pain every single day and did not know what it was like not to be in pain; everything hurt.

She moved through the emotional hurt and pain, writing powerful letters directed to her parents individually, pouring out exactly how she felt, all the stuff she could never voice, all the upset, all the hurt, all the anger and rage. She burned those letters afterwards, which truly helped shift the energy; everything changed.

After the letters and deep visualisation work to blast through the cysts and fibroids (she used a sword in her imagination to cut through the thick brambles and thorns), Karen noticed an immediate change in her periods; they became regular and effortless. All the pain of holding on, all the pain of inner crying went away, even the resentment of having her period vanished. Her face softened, her perspective changed, her thoughts changed, her feelings about her parents changed; therefore, the actual physical pain and medical conditions changed and left too. Her smile returned. She connected with her inner happiness, which radiated out; her posture changed, everything changed. She became pregnant naturally and found herself loving every second of pregnancy, delivered her baby with ease, and has a beautiful baby girl today who she feels is a true blessing in her life.

"All the struggle was worth it to be in this beautiful place of gratitude in my life now," she wrote. "Thank you, Jennifer, for helping me heal, for guiding me and believing in me. You are a true angel; xxx"

Abuse

The seat of all forms of abuse (physical, mental, emotional, or sexual) is in the womb. Your suppressed internalised pain and secrets are held tightly beneath the surface, tucked away in a heavy box, ornately carved and designed; this box contains shuddering, deep emotions, impatiently straining to become free. The fear of opening that box may be sickening, but I promise you, once acknowledged, once changed. Know that you are not delving into anything, I'm right here with you. It takes courage and great inner strength to acknowledge, change, or open that box. You have great inner strength. Nothing from the past has to define your future. Choose now to take your power back, and choose to work with whatever is buried or hidden.

You have the courage and strength to do it. You are ready to take back your power. Feel your strength. Feel your determination. You are taking back your power from that situation right now by choosing to acknowledge, change, or open the box. Your intuition will guide you to the best healing option for you. Please know, no matter what surfaces, you are ready to heal it. Let those shuddering emotions rush out, no longer uncontainable; you have your power back. Feel your power wash over you; feel it flow through you.

Feel the warmth from the beam of light shining upon you that acknowledging that box brings. Know you are only looking back to see how far you have come in life and to set yourself free. You are not delving into or dwelling on anything. You are reclaiming your life, your trapped energy, and your future. Now choose to discard that box in any way that feels right for you: smash it, break it, recycle it, repurpose it. Profound, deep, immense healing and freedom are yours now. You will enjoy these irreversible, wonderful changes throughout every aspect of your life. Sense and feel the instant lightness and brightness this brings you.

Allow the stepping stones to unfold before you. Had that not happened, you would not have met a certain person; you would not have done certain things or experienced XYZ. See your path highlight and unfold before you now; because of all you have experienced in life, you are the incredible person you are today. A huge burden and weight have been lifted. You are free. Once it's acknowledged, that heavy, ornately carved box is gone forever.

Lovemaking that was painful before now feels so deep; the change is dramatic. Everything changes now: how you feel, how you view the world. The freedom of letting those secrets go is profound, to say the least. Hear the phrase echo throughout your being: *They were coming from the best place they knew how.* This power-filled phrase will be your saving grace. Extend forgiveness now to those who have hurt you, physically, mentally, or emotionally. Forgiveness is not about them; it is solely about you, your freedom, your self-worth. You are stepping forward to become the incredible parent you know in your heart and soul to be. The release, the freedom, the space, and the room created for your baby are worth it.

You are worth it.

Adoption

Adoption is one of the most wonderful, beautiful things in this world; a family, a loving couple opened their hearts and home to you. They chose you, they wanted you so badly that they offered to share everything they have in this world with you, but immense hidden feelings of grief, loss, and despair are entangled with a deep-seated need to know who you are, where you come from. These feelings may even block you from feeling all that love and support surrounding you in your life.

You may have gone through life up to now feeling lost, not fully accepted, or misunderstood; this may have created inner blocks, resulting in you not loving, approving, or accepting yourself. This leads to constantly seeking and searching, asking, "Who am I? Where did I come from?" All this uncertainty only leads to more unanswered questions, playing havoc in the background. Confidence and trust become a great issue in your life. Intimacy is frequently difficult for you because of deep feelings of rejection, guilt, and shame. You don't have a true identity and subconsciously push others away to avoid experiencing another loss, which maybe masked by your big bubbly personality, laughing things off as a way of hiding true inner emotions of sadness, anger, resentment, and shame. These emotions frequently appear as a tangible presence in your work, relationships, and friendships. Shame causes a flood of stress hormones and a variety of biochemical reactions in your body, none of which feel positive, nourishing, or empowering.

Your body responds to your thoughts; what you believe affects every aspect of your life, whether you want it to or not. Confidence and trust are qualities you must claim for yourself. Now is the time to allow those old redundant barriers in the back of your mind, pain or unexplained weight gain, to dissolve, melt away, and drain out so you can advance confidently in the direction of your dreams.

For all intents and purposes, the experiences of your life can be turned around completely for your own radical well-being, because of your adoption and how you felt growing up; taking everything into consideration, you are the perfect person to lovingly have a baby, to lovingly accept your child for who they are, as they are. Erase those hidden fears of thinking you may not be able to bond with your own child, the way you thought your birth mother could not with you. You know firsthand how important feeling accepted is, and most importantly, you know you will be that beautiful, accepting, loving person in your child's life. It starts right here, right now with your thoughts: *I love and approve of myself.*

I love and approve of myself. I lovingly approve of and accept myself. Repeat again. Hear those words echoing in your mind and filter down to the core of your being.

Let's just take in a big, big breath now, and exhale fully all the way out.

Just breathing in.

Just breathing out.

Taking a moment to simply tune into your body,

Slow your breath down.

Allow your breath and awareness to pour into every cell and muscle of your body.

Recall to mind, a time in your life when you felt lost, uncertain, or ashamed.

What do you notice?

Do you feel like you want to shrink, curl, or retract in some way?

Do you avoid eye contact or the gaze of others?

Do you notice a variety of unpleasant sensations such as a hot flush, irritation on your skin, a pricking or painful sensation of discomfort, or nausea?

Just breathing in, just breathing out.

Now see these sensations as an image; what does it look like?

What is the first impression or image that pops in?

Change the image however it needs to be changed; your trusted subconscious knows the answer and how to change the image,

Or if it feels a little challenging right now, just imagine the sensation changing into a great big bunch of bright colourful balloons; feel yourself holding onto the strings, then give yourself full permission to open your hands and let them go.

Feel what that feels like; see those balloons being carried away in the breeze; follow the journey of the balloons, and in the distance see a group of children playing.

Notice one child spots the balloons, giggles, and points them out to the others.

Now see all the children point up towards the balloons with a great big smile on their faces, shouting with joy to the other kids in the playground.

Hear the sound of their laughter and excitement.

See the joy and happiness this release has brought to someone else; feel the joy and happiness of that great big release in your own body.

Immerse yourself in this joy, happiness, confidence, and trust.

You did it; you have made a huge shift towards your own endeavours.

Just breathing in, just breathing out as you echo those phrases in your mind again: "I lovingly approve of and accept myself; I lovingly approve of and accept myself."

Stand confident and strong in this new-found belief, with a whole new insight and innate knowingness; because of your adoption, you know the true value of being loved and accepted. You will excel at loving and wholeheartedly accepting your child for who they are, exactly as they are. Feel the essence of that new-found reassurance melt down any old fear of not being able to bond with your child, the way you once thought your birth mother could not with you. You understand now; something deep within you has changed and shifted. Send gratitude to this blessed reassurance; because of all you have experienced, you are empowered to know in your heart and soul you are an amazing parent. That is a powerful inner knowing in your own life, and you are worthy to receive your dreams.

Abortion

According to afterabortion.org, 92 per cent of people who had abortions reported that they experienced "emotional deadening." This is true for every case I have encountered; this may also be true for you, consciously or unconsciously. When you choose to have an abortion, there is always a sense of "that was my only option" for the situation. That is true; you were coming from the best place you knew how, with the knowledge and understanding you had at that time. You were doing the best you could to survive. Perhaps a logical decision was made, which was set so rigidly in concrete, it allowed no room for your emotions to be heard, and it asked if you would make the same decision again; absolutely, every single time, the answer is almost always instantly yes, validating how set in logical concrete that choice was.

This extreme decision, set in concrete, accompanied with emotional deadening, might be a crucial factor on your journey today, even though it may be years and years later, even though you are in a wonderful relationship right now, even though you are now ready to bring a baby into this world. The trapped emotional trauma of that time in your life has been stifled and left unresolved, leading to heavy emotions such as fear, guilt, resentment, and self-criticism.

The vulnerability of facing these emotions can often be too much to deal with; therefore, they are protected by a high degree of secrecy, deeply hidden in a top-secret compartment, lodged in the emotional home of your body: your womb. The fear of others, especially your current partner, learning of the abortion is a heavy weight to bear. The emotional effects of an abortion are intense and contribute to many painful gynecological symptoms.

The fight-or-flight element of the subconscious mind protects this information. You fear that disclosure could result in grave danger; therefore, it is tucked away, unresolved, unheard, and sealed tightly. This needs to be acknowledged so it can be released out of your subconscious mind and especially released out of your womb. But it doesn't have to be a struggle; it doesn't have to be difficult. Those aching, haunting old fears in the background can just come up and go.

You are choosing here to acknowledge in order to release and let go, not to delve into or dwell on anything; you are choosing to create the space you need to welcome your baby into your world and, most importantly, to set yourself free from this inner jail, be it known or unknown.

Please know and appreciate that babies come from a place of pure unconditional love; they rejoice in it and love unconditionally, regardless of the circumstances. They do not harbour hatred or resentment. Every single client I have encountered who has experienced a termination brings with them a very special loving gift; sitting on their left shoulder is the guiding presence of their baby. Yours is there too, shining a loving, angelic light. They carry nothing but pure unconditional love for you; there is not a trace of hatred or guilt towards you. If you are afraid there is, I promise you there is none. So if you harbour those feelings for yourself, now is the time for loving kindness, forgiveness, and self-love.

See their angelic light within now dissolving, melting away, all the way away. It's time now to completely release that fear, hatred, or resentment you have being holding. Feel their angelic loving presence; feel their light dissolving the guilt buried in your chest, allowing love to replace fear, allowing worthiness to be received, to override subconscious feelings of a need to be punished. You were coming from the best place you knew how at the time.

> See yourself walk free from jail now.
> Walk to freedom, step by step.
> What does it look like?
> What does it feel like?
> Feel gratitude for this experience to finally set yourself free.
> Feel the anticipation as your release grows imminent.
> Feel the explosion of love and joy as it radiates out from your heart.
> You are free to have a baby.
> You are free to be free. You are free; you are worthy to be a loving parent.

Three Bs of Infertility

Betrayal, Bitterness, Bereavement

Betrayal

Betrayal is the ultimate loss of trust or violation of confidence. You put your trust in someone, a close relationship or perhaps amongst individuals you work with, but your expectations fall vastly short. That loss of trust creates a tug of war, a moral and physiological conflict with yourself, initiating devastation, despair, and great pain within your physical body.

Betrayal is one of the most painful human experiences; discovering someone you trusted has hurt you pulls the reality rug from under you, leaving you feeling devastated and deeply upset. Betrayal lands you at a crossroad. You can choose to use this experience as an opportunity for personal growth, but all too often, you find yourself on the road to mistrust. Not trusting yourself, not trusting your judgement; your relationships and friendships come under scrutiny, keeping you stuck in torment and a bad moment in time forever, if you allow it.

Betrayal is one of those situations where you suffer in silence through disloyalty from a partner, friend, or family member. Your trust in others also erodes, which embeds deep, harmful emotions into the core of your being. If your best friend deceives you, you begin to think all friends are capable of this sinister act. The wounds of betrayal can be so submerged in your subconscious that they affect your relationship with others and also cause damage to the relationship with your own body.

When you hear the word *betrayal*, no doubt you immediately think of an affair. Betrayal comes in many forms: abandonment, vicious gossip, spreading lies, all of which contribute to heavy sickening feelings of sadness, anger, uncertainty, emotional pain, hurt, heartfelt sorrow, regret. The initial shock of something coming out of the blue lodges in your system, almost as if time stood still; that shock often resembles a black hole in the womb, cutting off the ebb and flow of life. Things build and fester in the mind and physical body. What once felt like solid trust suddenly crumbles; it is easy to succumb to the role of victim. This devastating mental turmoil creates a growing resentment deep within, resulting in physical lumps, bumps, cysts, and fibroids.

I fully understand the pain and turmoil you are in, but I would like to extend an invitation of self-exploration, an invitation to being open to the idea that perhaps you had a part to play, that perhaps on some level, you helped create the climate for betrayal. This empowering realisation offers you the hope of returning to that crossroad and taking the other route in the trusted reassurance of a resolution and healing to take place. You can begin the process of melting the deep resentment held within, which is no fun and has brought nothing but pain and suffering. You are worth more than that; I know you long for trust and true happiness back in your life.

You are ready to finally face the fears you've been ignoring; look them straight in the eyes now, and acknowledge your inner hurt. Allow those feelings to be heard and respected. Go to a mirror, and look directly into your own eyes; it may feel challenging to actually do that, but I promise you, it is worth it. It will open the door to your longed-for healing. Loving yourself is the most powerful thing you can do right now; I want you to appreciate one thing in the mirror you like and love about yourself.

Use the mirror work to communicate in a more authentic way with yourself, first and foremost, then you will be able to communicate better with others. All this pain is like a red flag waving, wanting your attention and acknowledgement; we usually do everything, take painkillers and pain suppressants, everything except listen. Being courageous and confronting the inevitable betrayal, abandonment, or rejections you have felt will help heal the hurt of your heart. See an image of your heart now in your mind's eye; what soothing compassion do you need? It's like a child who falls and scrapes their knee, and the mother lovingly rubs it better. Do that to you heart now; soothe it with compassion. Be kind to yourself and towards your pain; develop a deeper understanding of it. Move towards growth, transformation, and the innate wisdom that resides within you and can guide you.

Loving and forgiving yourself are the fastest ways of digging up, wiping away, and clearing out old memories, worn-out, played-out thoughts holding you back, keeping you stuck and stagnant. Forgive yourself, and understand that the other person and you were coming from the best place you knew how, with the knowledge you had at that time. Forgiveness does not affirm that what they did or said was right; it's about setting yourself free of the stronghold grip of the past. It is certainly not about accepting the wrong behaviour. Forgiveness breaks you free from pain, turmoil, anger, frustration, and bitterness buried within. Set yourself free now.

Bitterness

Bitterness is a multilayered emotion, a mixture of disappointment, anger, fear, and disgust. All bitterness starts out as a small hurt that's held onto and festers under the surface. That festering hurt forms into contempt, which begins to govern your thinking, distorting your beliefs, creating intense antagonism, clouding your mind and judgement. Bitterness is a deep feeling of resentment which encompasses both anger and hatred. It consumes you and leaves an unpleasant, bitter taste of unhappiness that's difficult to comprehend. Bitterness results from clinging tightly to negative experiences; it eats you up inside. Bitterness and resentment are like drinking poison yourself and expecting someone else to die.

These heavy emotions destroy you and your future happiness. They zap the joy from your life and soul. I would suggest absolutely acknowledging and releasing any held bitterness to fulfil your own dreams of becoming a parent. When bitterness is suppressed, you cannot help but feel bitter towards others who share their joyful news; it just wells up from nowhere. Even though you want to be happy, this undertone of bitterness sneaks up on you and throws you completely off balance, leaving you feeling irritable and out of sorts.

Imagine the news swirling around that someone is pregnant; it is heart-wrenching at worst, unsettling at best. *When will it be my turn?* you hear echo in your mind. *What's wrong with me? Everyone's pregnant.* You look out the window; even the neighbour's cat sitting on the wall is pregnant. The joy, the happiness, the bitterness (they weren't even trying), the hope, the frustration, the anger, and eventually the sadness prevails.

Belief determines perception: "I'm flawed. I was an accident and not wanted. I'll never amount to anything" because of whatever past mistake or limited beliefs ingrained that you are unworthy to go forward in life and be happy. Have you ever found yourself in a similar barrage, a cycle of ill feelings and emotions? The bitterness of "I'm not good enough" stays underwater; intrinsically, you do not love yourself. You find yourself in a constant state of criticism, criticising yourself and others; so much noise and clutter of the mind and emotions.

You're haunted by unspoken expectations, wearing a mask, a facade of false pretense, blocking out affection, attention, love; seeking out criticism and situations that only reinforce those beliefs. Acknowledge them now and ask why. Be willing to look at your belief systems; be willing to become emotionally balanced. You are not the child being ridiculed anymore. Parents or adults make general sweeping statements; sometimes, as a child, it might have felt as though you were not good enough or not worthy. Understand, parents are coming from the best place they know how; they would go to the end of the earth to keep their child safe. As a child, you have no clue of that; you are on the other end of that fear of something happening to you. This fear has been hanging over you, at a high cost, until now. Beliefs determine the outcomes of your life. Stop and ask yourself, who are you angry at? What are you bitter about?

Tune into your body, and notice where you feel bitterness in it. Who or what was the first impression that popped up? What does that bitterness feel like for you? Allow whatever is ready to surface to arise. Neither willfully create nor suppress your feelings; make a list, write them down, give a voice to these suppressed twisted, knotted, and intertwined feelings.

Dump it all out onto a page; connect the dots. Mistakes are just learning opportunities; rid yourself of judgements. See your vulnerabilities; let there be a degree of peace around the idea of not having to be the perfect person all the time. Self-esteem comes from the inside; embrace your confidence, body, identity, relationship. Look back now on that situation only to see how far you have come; you are a strong driving force in life.

Now see the initial hurt as just a grievance and not the belief you had once interpreted; find meaning and purpose in your life. Let your wound guide you to growth. The pain was stuffed down; you needed to shield yourself at that time. Gather your strength, and rip the bitterness out. I know you don't want to look at it. There's no need to; just throw it in the bin, physically. Grab the bitterness from wherever it is in your body and dump it in the trash or wash it down the sink. How did that feel? I bet you feel lighter and freer now.

Constantly looking for external recognition has not worked; constant criticism of yourself hurts, only adding to your wound. Shielding causes more trapped pain to fester, like poking at a wound. Perfectionism perhaps shielded your anger. Maybe you have a sense of walking on eggshells, on tenterhooks, awaiting the next negative thing to happen or the next thing to control.

Estranged relationships, being invisible, avoiding attention, or people pleasing are perhaps prominent in your life. You serve everyone else's needs before your own. You feel unworthy of love and are willing do anything to get people to like you. You want to be perfect, to experience gratification, but feel nothing but sadness when things go unnoticed. You feed your feelings of "I'm not good enough," your worries, and your fears.

It all comes back to self-love; you cannot be angry or jealous if you are in a great, happy place in your life. Now think of someone you love and adore, someone who brings an instant smile to your face the moment you think of them or hear their name. Feel the immense happiness they bring you. Hold that happiness, and try to be angry. Could you get angry?

You get to choose whether you stay in a place of bitterness or move to a place of happiness. Just remember the face of someone you love, a pet, favourite pair of shoes, whatever brings joy and happiness to you. In an instant, with one thought, you can take yourself out of unhappiness.

Grow and evolve, no matter how many years have gone by; unpack this story from your psyche. Release the trauma and bitterness from you and the other person. It holds you back; energetically heal the relationship. Visualise giving them a white flower; you can even leave it on their doorstep if handing it is too much. Say goodbye and thank you. Your personal healing and freedom are what's important now. Create empathy and understanding.

View this opportunity as a gift; your deepest wound is the source of the greatest gift you can receive in this world. You have endured enough. It's time to overcome it; otherwise, you run the risk of becoming a victim to your own sabotaging beliefs. Allow love to flow in. Allow trust to flow in. You get to choose this freedom. You get to choose trust, which is your ultimate protection; reach your tipping point to simply allow this ultimate changing experience.

Now, take the list of feelings and mistake, and burn that page. Transmute those old feelings, and free that trapped energy. Change your circumstances completely into something brighter and better. Feel the freedom and release this brings you. Notice the difference in your breath. Notice the difference in your physical body.

Just pause; find a nice breath.
Just silently breathe; find a deeper breath.
Take in a big, beautiful breath.
Exhale fully, all the way out.

Now, in this moment, begin to connect to the opposite of noise, the stillness.
Allow that stillness to spread.
Begin to feel feelings you have not felt in a while: stillness, peace, quietness.
Feel the peace; feel the feelings of possibility, of hope, of trust and belief.

Underneath all that noise and chaos reside hope and possibility.
Envelop yourself in deep hope, deep trust in yourself.
Trust in your body.
Trust your own capabilities.
You've got this.

Now plant the seeds in your heart, in your body, in your life.
As you nurture it, it grows.
It strengthens.
It becomes the stillness of the moment, the wisdom, the peace, the joy, the happiness, the gratitude.
The hope is who you are.
You've got this.

Bereavement

Bereavement is the period of grief following the death of a family member or a friend, the loss of a job, anything that has a substantial impact on your life and well-being. Bereavement is composed of sadness, emotional numbness, crying, distorted sleep patterns, depression, regret, and other heavy, negative feelings. It can come in waves.

The passing of a loved one is one of the greatest sorrows that can occur in your life, especially when coping with the loss of a parent as you embark on your journey to pregnancy. You may find it hard to accept that the loss has occurred in the first place and find it just as hard to adjust to becoming a parent without the support of your own mother or father. Maybe you've always envisioned how your parents would be around to love and adore your children and spoil them rotten, in that special way only a grandparent can do.

Emotions may be very intense, filled with guilt and sentiments of "I should have …," "I could have …," or "I wish I had …." The loss of a parent can have a deep impact, no matter what age you are when it occurs, whether you believe it was their time to go or not. The loss of your parent may also mean the loss of your best friend, your go-to person, the person you wish was here with you now; this may leave you feeling very much alone.

Please know that they are still with you, encouraging you, loving you, supporting you; it's just in a different way. If you place your hand on your heart right now and ask them a question, I guarantee you will hear their voice; listen to their encouragement and guidance now. They want this for you, as much as you do yourself. You will always be able to hear their advice and see their smile; they will always be in your heart. Nothing can ever take your cherished memories and fond moments away. Feel this new connection in your heart. Smile when you think of them.

Know that your loved ones came into your life to bring you joy and happiness, to guide and teach you, to help you grow and flourish; they did not come into your life to leave you in the depths of despair. Remember now, in the most beautiful way, their smile, their laughter, a funny joke they told, a funny thing they did, how they inspired and supported you; allow these fond memories to flood your mind now. Feel your heart overflow with joy and happiness.

If a not-so-fond image surfaces, acknowledge where it is; did you see it right in front of your face? Was it off to the side of your vision? Was it on the right side or left side? Now catch that image, crumple it up, and throw it away. Replace it with another happy image of a cherished time in your life. Set an intention that only happy thoughts and memories are allowed from now on. Crumple and throw away any others; see a wonderful image—a favourite trip, holiday, or special occasion—and remember the joy. Remember the fine details. Feel your strength in taking back your power. Confidently know that your loved ones are right there by your side; they've got your back, encouraging you every step of the way. Feel their presence; feel their supporting hug. Smile. They want to see your beautiful smile. It always brings them great joy to see you happy.

The loss of a long-term romantic partner is also challenging. Any loss or passing is devastating; it is especially traumatic if the person passed at a young age or soon after you got married. You committed to spend your life with them and possibly wanted to have children with them. This loss is huge and insurmountable, incomprehensible on many levels.

It's crucial to identify the emotions connected to your loss and see where they are anchored in your body.

Coping with a great loss is painful and exhausting; it often feels easier to avoid confronting these feelings so they get pushed down, knitted, and stitched into the lining of your womb.

Conceiving after losing a loving partner or a child can be burdensome, to say the least. The struggle is enormous, punishing, and almost grueling. It's baffling and confusing to be pulled in different directions. Haunting memories drag you into the past; anxiety-ridden fears tormenting your future. It is wearing and bittersweet; you wish to have another baby, but the guilt of replacing a baby who passed can be perplexing. Then there are the fears of what if something happens to this baby; your poor body, mind, and heart are torn, emotionally devastated, and mentally overwhelmed, regardless of the time frame that may have passed. The loss of a child is the ultimate loss for any parent.

Do you hold an overwhelming sense of injustice for unfulfilled dreams, lost potential?

Do you blame yourself and feel responsible for your child or partner passing?

I suggest you gently place your hand on your heart and ask your child or partner, "Do you blame me?"

I guarantee you'll hear, "No, I only have love for you," from your loved one. Your cherished loved one is in a beautiful, serene place of pure peace; there is no pain, suffering, anger, resentment, or blame. Those feelings are part of this world and not the next. Only peace, gratitude, and love prevail; know that wholeheartedly, and allow yourself to feel immersed in that prevailing peace also.

Allow yourself in this moment to let go of the blame you put on yourself. Give yourself full permission to let go of this heavy burden. Rest assured that there is nothing you could have said or done that would have changed the outcome of the situation. Your cherished loved one loves you infinitely. They want you to be happy; they give you full permission to be happy. Feel that, know that, and please believe that.

Give yourself a great big hug right now. Send huge gratitude to yourself. You are doing brilliantly. Discover your road map to becoming a parent in a holistic yet profound way. You have taken some hard steps on your journey. Congratulations on your determination for coming this far. I truly commend you. Now that you have acknowledged some hidden emotional wounds, let's step forward and heal them.

Freedom from Inner Guilt

Feeling Unworthy

We are created to be free. Freedom resides deep within you. This freedom will not intrude; it will not force you to embrace it.

Its invitation, like the gentle whisper of your intuition, is subtle and gracious. In order to inherit and claim your freedom, you must go within; you have to go towards it. You have to seek out the inner roadblocks impeding you on this journey, by acknowledging the learned behaviours and beliefs that no longer serve you well. This beautiful gift of freedom is yours, should you choose to acknowledge and take it.

We all have a reservoir of unknown freedom; you have a source of freedom ready to be tapped into, yet your fears hold you back. The heaviest chains that cut the deepest, those shackles around your ankles holding you back, are not the ones others would have you wear, but the ones you tied on yourself, thinking you are not good enough or believing there is something wrong with you. There isn't.

Those are the fears that hold the longest and have the biggest impact on this journey. You cannot control what others do or say, but you can certainly control how you react and respond; you can even control how you make yourself feel. You stepped into that prison of unworthiness, guilt, lack, expectation, stress, worry, anxiety yourself, whichever prison you are trapped in, but the great news is that you can step out of that prison. You can rise above blame, go beyond excuses, and land into freedom.

It is awful to feel unworthy or guilty; your body, your mind, your spirit become haunted. You keep returning to some event of the past, the scalpel of a sentence, a word from another, maybe it was something your doctor said: "You have 1 per cent chance of becoming pregnant," "You will never hold your own baby in your arms," that cut deep into your psyche. You are holding onto that now; don't allow it in.

Pull up the anchor on that statement, that word, that look, whatever it was that haunts you, and set yourself free. You deserve to feel worthy. You deserve to experience happiness. There is nothing you cannot overcome; you deserve to be a parent. You deserve to discover, learn from, and overcome any obstacle in your way. You are meant to be free, not stuck; do not allow any bleak prognosis to filter into your body, mind, or energy.

Let's ponder on that mere "1 per cent chance" for a moment and put it into perspective; on average, women are born with two million eggs, and men have millions of sperm per ejaculation. you do the math: 1 per cent of two million is still a lot, and it only takes one egg and one sperm to make a baby.

All this focus on the numbers that are declining, but what about all the eggs and sperm? They are not declining; it only takes one egg and one sperm to get pregnant, and with the right mindset shift, anything and everything is possible.

Challenges in life are there to help you grow, not to stop you in your tracks. Imagine a huge bolder in your path; how do you choose to overcome it? You should know that there is always a way; you can roll it off the cliff, you can blast through it, you can go around it, you can tunnel under it, or you can climb over it. You can even have fun and abseil down the other side.

No one lives a perfect life; everyone has some burdensome secret. Visit the corner of your heart now; allow it to reveal to you the trapped emotional wound in the background. Invite this unworthiness in whatever form it is to reveal itself and come alive, and then ask yourself, "Is it truthful? Is it kind? Is it even valid or worthy anymore?" I bet the answers are no, no, no; therefore, delete, delete, delete.

Sometimes, we hold things from the past that should hold no bearing on us now, just because you felt bad about something at one time and exaggerated it. You should know that it is useless now. It belongs to the past, and the past is over and done now. Regardless of how bad you feel, you cannot return to that time; when a past event becomes a continuous cloud over your life, you are locked in an emotional prison, destroying your future happiness.

Taking your power back is such a great moment of liberation. When you learn to forgive yourself, life forgives you; walk out now, dance, skip, or hop onto a new path of promise and infinite possibilities, filled with self-compassion. It's a wonderous gift to give yourself; give it to yourself right now. Commit to never return to that haunted fixation again. Commit to excitement; feel your eyes fill with childlike adventure, curiosity, wonder, and awe. Learn the art of integrating your faults; they are part of who you are. Learn to integrate them, to begin your journey of healing, of overcoming, of holding your head up high.

May you receive the healings and blessings you need and deserve for your greater good.

May you be free from inner and outer turmoil.

May you have an abundance of health, joy, and happiness.

Joy

Remember what joy is, even during turbulent and challenging times, when you may be having trouble turning off your busy, anxious mind and experiencing restless nights. Remember to feel and experience joy, a feeling of great pleasure and happiness. Take delight in all things, especially the small things we take for granted, learning to live in the treasure house of your own being, your beautiful body. Tap into the vast possibilities and capabilities that are truly yours on this adventure that is your life.

But how do you keep your passion, excitement, and enthusiasm all going and ignited on this journey? The answer is joy.

Friends, please know, you deserve to be happy; you deserve to be filled with a sense of well-being and purpose. You deserve to take delight in all things and feel joyously alive.

Yes, much misery may have prevailed in your journey thus far, but perhaps the time has come to lift it off so life can breathe and move more freely. Your own sense of buoyant joy comes first; cast off the dark clouds of pain and discomfort. Transform your energy through clarity and focus. See joy and happiness in everything, in each and every moment. See the essential truth that joy is the primary element in all creation.

Learn to recognise yourself as an energy being in the purest of joy. Ask yourself, "How can I be happy in the presence of suffering?" Even in the midst of your own suffering, you can still experience joy. It is possible to feel the power of joy pulsing through your life. Joy does not deny the presence of pain or suffering; they are part of life. It does not pretend to ignore sorrow. Joy is far greater than an emotion; it is a state of being, giving you energy, vitality, and enthusiasm to follow through with projects, plans, dreams, and purpose.

Each joyous step of life is like walking on a lotus blossom, moving from one beautiful petal to another. Each step leads you to new ways of feeling fulfilled, of seeing the bigger picture, and of understanding; all can be experienced, even when things are not perfect.

The path of joy is a keen awareness, filled with pleasure and goodness on all levels. Joy is integrated into everything; it is the foundation of creation. Practicing joy increases an ever-fulfilling wave of happiness which flows out into the world; allow joy to be linked with these words: *trust, pregnancy, baby.* It is a wonderful force, stimulating and creating more of itself. Joy has the capacity to constantly increase and bring more joy and happiness into your life.

People's authentic version of joy is unique to them, so look within yourself now; what is your sense of the reality of joy? Learn to recognise and celebrate its presence. We are all hungry for more energy, vitality, and well-being, more gladness in our lives. Yet we wonder how it is even possible to consider living in a state of joy when the world is so grievously overrun by pain.

Find the balance of living, and see the happiness joy brings, being mindful not to ignore times of personal suffering while pretending to be happy and joyous. Instead, joy and happiness can live simultaneously with pain; even during times of authentic pain, joy has the power to transmute that suffering.

Living in a state of deep joy will bring more compassion, trust, and faith than you might otherwise attain. We need to remember a truth about excess suffering: It debilitates you and may even persuade you that life is meant to be painful. Many of us have been taught that you must suffer, struggle, or work hard for everything you have. We believe that things cannot come easy, but the reality is, they can.

The absence of a rich desire for life and joy is one of the very reasons so many people are sick, sick in mind, sick in body, and sick in spirit. Discovering the power of joy enables you to melt, dissolve, and drain some of life's sufferings away, coming instead to a keen awareness of the happiness life offers. Don't wait to have your baby to experience joy and happiness; feel it now.

Practice joy and gratitude daily; release the burden of anguish. Make joy a light-hearted practice; establish an awareness from the moment you awaken each day. Minute by minute, hour by hour, day by day; this will help you to discover and transmute any cloud of pain into an energy of mindful delight.

You can then participate in the co-creation and co-design of your own life.

You have far more power on this path than you realise. Surround yourself with happiness; leave all groups and forums that are filled with negativity, gossip, or despair. Provide yourself with more energy, passion, and excitement. Be filled with new ideas.

Start with joyful thoughts and beliefs; let them be a river of faith and trust. Let them flow freely into all aspects of your life. We are wired for happiness, and when you live within that belief, you experience great peace of mind. Commit to expressing and filling your awareness with pure joy. Become aware of all its visitations; store them in your heart, and feel them playing throughout your physical body.

Observe your pets or the animal kingdom for inspiration. Our dog Belle is so funny; she lives with great passion, expressing that joyous delight by wagging her tail the moment she sees us pick up the car keys. Such exuberance is expressed through her eyes, and there's no question about her desires: "I'm coming with you for a spin."

Look for it in the butterfly that flitters past, the purring of a cat being rubbed. Savour your meals; relish the pleasures of life. Enjoy a child's smile, the sound of laughter. Perfect the art of maximising and exuding joy, even when days are hard. There is joy in the touch of light, the sound of music; connect to the beauty all around you, and simply allow your consciousness to alleviate any stress, worry, or tension. As each succeeding moment holds the illumination of joy, it can be extended forth to a joyful expectation, joyful pregnancy; you should know that joy is always moving towards you.

Feel joyful acceptance and acknowledgement; surround yourself with people, events, and pleasures that demonstrate the sweetness of life. Allow gratitude and praising others to become a way of being; it need not be overdone but rather filled with grace from deep within.

Take each element of delight fully into your body, mind, and heart so that your feelings. your organs, your bones are strengthened, and your ideas are infused with joy. Draw your joy in through your eyes, circulate it around in your blood, feed your ears with joy. Taste joy in your mouth through kindness in your speech. Breathe in joy through your nose, and feel your thoughts immersed. Absorb joy in through your skin; feel it flow through your spine.

Acknowledge joy by writing, singing, and dancing, and send it out in all directions by reading it aloud. Be dedicated to this wonderful feeling; become conscious and aware of your patterns that drown your joy, and sabotage yourself, or zap your happiness. Move through them and overcome them by taking joyful action. Bring yourself into alignment with the core values of joy, pleasure, and happiness. Observe and notice their profoundness. Have a sense of joy for others, no matter how you are feeling. Babies are magnets to joy and happiness.

When you think about it, what is the first thing you do when you see a baby? Before you even realise it, you are smiling from ear to ear; no matter how bad you are feeling, they always bring that smile out from you.

Smile, love, and be happy; now, no more waiting.

Part 2

Emotional Wounds

Fertility Present

Your Fertility Present

Are you subconsciously sabotaging conception and your desires?

It probably seems like you could not be in a worst situation right now; you want your baby, but you are deep in struggle and filled with self-doubt. You want harmony, but you are excruciating pain each day. It feels like life is telling you, "No way; you cannot have it." But you should know that is not true; you can. Your dream is available and attainable to you, even though the reality may feel like the total opposite.

But every dream comes with built-in challenges; they are designed that way to help us grow and learn. This is how we evolve in life; it does not mean you have a more difficult road ahead; this is the journey. You can be dealing with devastation and pain, but you can work your way through it. You can be feeling sad and lonely but still move towards the path of joy and happiness.

You knew the probabilities and still chose to be a mother; you are not at a disadvantage. You are on your path, on your way there; positive results are experienced, despite fears to the contrary. Even though you are in pain or feel like a failure, you can still become pregnant. No matter long you have been on this journey, you can still become pregnant.

If circumstance show up that oppose your dream, simply acknowledge them and say hello; do not feed into negativity and doubt. How can you act when there is so much confusion about what you want? You want a baby but secretly think, *This month is not great; I have a big work project on, and next month, we have a wedding. The month after, there is something else.* You don't know which way to go. How can your body and mind be on the same page of certainty when you are too afraid to believe?

But there will always be something to be afraid of; there will always be something to take precedence if you allow it. Even though you have a wedding next month, you can still become pregnant and enjoy the wedding. Even though you have projects on in work, you can still become pregnant and get the work done, even if you got started on a rocky road, thinking, *I don't have all the resources I need; I am still terrified of pregnancy. Parenthood seems daunting sometimes. I still don't have confidence; my past was awful. I'll just wait for a miracle or immaculate conception.*

Miracles don't just come to you; miracles will find you on your rocky path, but you have to act. Change the "I can't" into "I can, I will, I am." Fill this phrase with depth, feeling and meaning.

Have you ever seen a mother duck and her babies in a row behind her? She does not wait for them all to line up first; she goes, and they fall into place, lining up behind her. Be the momma duck in your life; step forward with certainty, even though you may not see your ducks assembled in a row behind you. You need to complete your journey, trusting and believing your ducks will fall into place. You may not see them, but you can trust that they are there.

Begin to sense an openness to the many possibilities that are available to you. See your eggs filled with joy, ready, willing, and able. They are delighted for this opportunity to be trusted. Begin to sense an openness to what is known and what is unknown, to what is familiar and what is unfamiliar, to the ups and the downs, to the ins and outs; each night is followed by another day.

As you ride the waves that rise and fall from one moment to the next, find a rhythm to this journey that guides you and soothes you, where the certainties and uncertainties blend together into a flow that is much like the ebb and flow of nature: the gentle lapping of the waves against the shoreline, where each sunrise is followed by a sunset. The breath flows in, and the breath flows out.

You did what you could with the resources you had. Even though you once felt like you are not ready, or you are not good enough, I can tell you that you are ready; you are good enough. Now is the perfect time. Even if you still feel the lingering doubt that you are not ready, go towards the end of the road, anyway. Feel the fear, and do it anyway. Get ready; this is happening. Now that you've refocused your mindset, your miracle will come towards you and meet you on your path.

The Big Why?

Now I would like you to connect to your big "Why?"

Why do you want to bring a child into this world?

Why is parenthood important for you?

So far, you've been consumed by "How can I get pregnant?" Now, I urge you to connect to why it's important to you.

Why do you want to be pregnant?

Why do you want to become a mother?

Why?

When you ask yourself these questions, observe what they inspire within you physically, mentally, and emotionally. Notice what thoughts come up as a result.

Why do you want this?

What will becoming a mother bring you? How will your life be different?

When you become a parent, what will be different as opposed to now?

When you connect deeply with your "why" and understand what it means for you, the "how and when" will be taken care of and presented to you.

Get crystal clear now.

Why do you want to become a parent?

Why?

I want to acknowledge you for showing up and commend you for being present with this inner work. I am very proud of you. I hope you are beginning to feel truly empowered; you should feel proud of yourself. I hope you are noticing some dawning awakenings, realisations, and aha moments surfacing.

Taking back your power on this journey is the most liberating experience you will most likely ever go through. Stop feeling bombarded with information; don't be overwhelmed. It can be really confusing and stressful. Become attuned with your intuition, and listen to its gentle whispers of guidance. Thank yourself for your attention, trust, and belief.

I encourage you now to confidently step into this present moment of empowerment. Visualise yourself reaching your arms out overhead and proclaiming to the universe, "I am confident, and I believe in myself."

Now visualise yourself pregnant; see what you see, feel what you feel, and hear what you hear. If you can see it in your mind's eye and feel it in your heart, you can experience pregnancy in this lifetime. See it. Feel it. Believe it. Do this every single day, numerous times a day, and before you know it, you will receive the positive results you deserve.

Having a positive fertility mindset is the most crucial thing you can do. Everything else will fall into place when your mindset is on the right track.

It is normal to be a little sceptical of new information and different techniques. Rest assured, there is method in my madness. I know how to help guide you in the right direction. I have personally worked with thousands of clients and have spent over a decade specialising in this area, working with clients from all kinds of backgrounds. I helped wonderful people like you to get positive results; not because I tell you what to do but because I guide you to step out of your own way. You succeed through your own inner work.

I am here for you all the way. I will not give up on you, so promise now not to give up on yourself.

You can be a mum right now, being exactly who you are, as you are. You do not need to lose weight, you do not need to be younger, and you do not need to be perfect. Yes, you will still have fears, but those fears will become less scary and far more manageable to deal with. We all fear we are not good enough, not perfect enough, or not ready, but let me tell you, you are ready, you are good enough, you are perfect right now, exactly as you are.

Trust you are developing new strengths and skills, conditioning your mindset with new confidence, enhancing communication with yourself, first and foremost, ensuring challenging fears are turned into opportunities for growth and understanding. You are no longer feeding your fears and worries. Instead, you are choosing to look them directly in the eye, seeing they are not so scary, after all. There is a solution to everything. There is always a way. Can you feel that mindset shift already?

Challenges are not meant to keep you stuck and stagnant; they are stepping stones to your joyous future. When viewed this way, anything and everything is possible.

Quick recap so far: We talked about your fertility past, how your mindset, beliefs, and fears get passed down, often subconsciously, through the generations by actions and behaviours, which brought your awareness to nuances you may never have thought of or connected to before.

I bet it felt liberating to finally realise why that one comment, phrase, or motto bothered you throughout the years, totally unbeknownst to you, until now. You now understand that you have the freedom to create your own legacy with a whole fresh new start. There's a blank canvas for your bright future.

You may also have experienced many aha moments drop into your awareness, old memories resurfacing that seemed normal to you growing up, but you now have a different perspective on how family habits or sayings impact you today. You might be wondering why it's so important to recognise those experiences; the past is the past, and bringing up your family's history may evoke feelings of unease, but maybe your family members, friends, or peers are constantly moaning and complaining about having children, saying how much they suffered through pregnancy or childbirth or how much they sacrificed. Even though they love their children, they may complain constantly about how tired they are. That undertone of sacrifice had a huge impact, and its effects are felt today.

Those complaining elements, listened to repetitively, will end up becoming your norm, if you allow them. Challenges do not have to be challenging; they can be great opportunities for growth and learning. Sacrifice does not have to leave you feeling as though you have lost out or are missing something; you can shift perspective and view this fabulous new stage of your life as adventurous and fun.

Difficulties do not have to be difficult. Change your thoughts, and change your world. I suggest you surround yourself with positive people who are radiant during pregnancy, who thrive in parenthood, who rejoice in this wonderful new phase of their lives. They, too, experience challenges, but instead of focusing on the challenges, they focus on growth and experiences.

The pleasure of having children is far greater and more prominent, allowing them to embrace whatever comes their way, letting go of sabotaging patterns of the past, be they known or unknown. They know it's okay to let go of the constant moaning of peers, colleagues, or friends. If you have felt lonely, isolated, or frustrated by the conversations you've been having with people in your life, you are really going to enjoy the release when you step away from heavy, negative conversations.

Nothing that happened to you in the past is your fault. Step out of the realm of blame and excuses by understanding that people were coming from the best place they knew how, with the resources they had available to them at the time.

You could not control the family or situation you were born into; you did not choose the country or city you grew up in. Nothing that happened to you in the past dictates or defines you or your future potential. Allow this to echo in your subconscious. People were coming from the best place they knew how, with the resources that they had available to them at the time. You now have this blessed opportunity to grow, to learn, and to evolve.

You have this blessed opportunity to set yourself free and create your own positive future by choosing to send loving kindness and forgiveness to your past, to all those who may have hurt you physically, mentally, or emotionally. They no longer have a hold on you. You are free to move forward. You are free to release the limiting beliefs you inherited that once held you back. Break free from the negative subconscious family lineage right now. You can still honour your ancestors.

Your great-grandmother would want you to experience it all: career, family, and great happiness. Your ancestors may not have had the opportunity of choice, but you do. Please know they are supporting you all the way. Listen to your ancestors cheering you on with encouragement. They want this for you as much as you want it for yourself. Believe that wholeheartedly.

Without this awareness, the past would have continued to influence your future subconsciously, but now you have the power, the power to release old limiting beliefs that no longer serve you well. You have the power to receive; you have the power to take care of yourself and your beautiful body. Release any past conditioning that did not feel right anyway.

The best news is that there are no rules anymore about who can or cannot have a baby. Teachers are no longer restricted by old-fashioned, outdated rules. A rule for teachers in 1914 was "You will not marry or have a baby during the term of your contract." A rule for teachers in 1872 was "Women teachers who marry or engage in improper conduct will be dismissed." Can you believe that? How interesting is this: In all my years working in this field, guess which profession has the highest number of clients experiencing fertility issues: teachers.

The result of this past conditioning is still having an effect in the world today, even though this is nonsense and has not been valid for years. I have encountered teachers whose teaching contracts still had reference to this; even though that section was crossed out, it was still there in black and white, and it was subconsciously impactful.

If you are a teacher, may I suggest you write up a new teaching contract for yourself, giving yourself full permission to thrive as a teacher and be a happy parent. After having this aha moment, realising the conditioning they've been living under, and signing their new contract, many of my clients became pregnant almost instantly. The power of the mind is so profound.

There are no rules anymore about who can and cannot have a baby. You can work and have a baby. You can be in a same-sex couple and have a baby. You can be single and have a baby. You can be sixteen, have a baby, and still go to school. You can even be in your forties and have a baby.

Imagine that; you can be in your forties, in the prime of your life, and enjoy a safe, healthy, happy pregnancy. Please don't include that dated medical term, geriatric mother. Ask your doctor to kindly refrain from referring to you as that. You cannot control those around you and what they think or say; if you hear that expression at an appointment, simply nod and smile and think in your mind, *I'm a cool and amazing mother,* instead. You cannot control things in the world; you cannot dismantle inequalities or discrimination, but you can control how you respond.

You can control your own thoughts and abilities. You can take responsibility for the decisions you make each and every day, going forward, including investing time in your mindset, which is what you are doing right now by doing the work in this book. It is never too late to change your thoughts and change your world. You are the perfect age to have a baby.

There is no time like the present to just take in a big, big breath. Add in those powerful words: inhaling sooooo, exhaling hmmmm. Feel your body responding by relaxing, calming, and refocusing. Feel better already. I am going to ask you, what brought you to this book, this work today? What's the first thing that pops into your mind? You are most likely tracking your monthly cycle, monitoring it like crazy, but are you celebrating your monthly cycle? Are you celebrating your period?

You're probably asking, what do you mean, am I celebrating my monthly cycle? Yes, celebrating: thanking your body for following and complying to what it has been asked to do. This is quite the revelation for most people; your body listens to your fears and protects you from them. Your body listens to the family's lineage, inherited beliefs, values, mottos (be they known or unknown) and complies with them, rebels against them, or feels suppressed by them. How much do you value and trust your body right now? On a scale from one to ten, how much do you trust your body right now (one being "not at all," ten being "I totally trust my amazing body")?

Your body follows every single command it is given. The problem is, we are usually sending it the wrong command, asking the opposite of what we actually want; are you consumed by thoughts of the very thing you do not want to experience: your period? Are you watching like a hawk, looking out for your period every time you use the bathroom, then getting upset when it shows up?

Imagine, for a moment, if you were not focusing on your period; what is the opposite? What could you focus on instead? A positive pregnancy test result. A safe, healthy, happy pregnancy. I will say this again; allow it to percolate in: "Your body listens to your fears and protects you from them."

If there is so much stress, fear, worry, and especially physical tension around having a baby or doing a pregnancy test, your body will red-flag those feelings; it will link together the words *baby, stress, fear.* Listen to this phrase again, and allow yourself to shift perspective to gratitude and understanding: In order to keep you safe, your body listens to your fears and will protect you from them; it is listening to all that fear, which is held in the subconscious, and feeling all those fiery emotions in your womb, which ultimately block pregnancy from happening, .

So please thank your body now, and please relieve it of its protection duty.

Now, vividly see the link of *baby, joy, happiness* in your mind's eye. Feel the physical tension in your body melting, dissolving, disappearing, or draining away. Most people operate from a have-do-be paradigm, thinking *If I have a baby and do all this sacrificing, then I will be happy.* They think, *I will be happy when I have my baby,* but that's backwards. It's actually the other way around: be-do-have—if you choose to behold the feelings of happiness you wish to experience when you have a baby, now, then you will organically do the right things and allow your body to confidently relax into trust and belief, and then you will have your baby before you know it.

You need to feel the happy feelings first so you can link and associate baby with happiness, rewiring from the current link of baby with stress and unhappiness to be-do-have: what you send out, you get back.

The worst enemy you could have is your own mind, especially if it is consumed by fear of the unknown. Imagine if you addressed this fear of the unknown right now and sent the opposite message to your subconscious mind and body. Send the message of what it is you actually want to experience. How different would that feel?

Imagine if you trusted your body, and your body responded to that trust by feeling safe and relaxed, and you ultimately welcomed pregnancy with open arms. Imagine if your body associated and linked together the words *baby, trust, happiness, joy*. How much nicer would that feel? Go back to that question, are you celebrating and thanking your body? Now can you see how vital that awareness is?

Your body is like a top student, your best friend following your lead and direction; up until now, you were completely unaware of this mental block, inhibiting you from seeing and understanding the effects your thoughts and beliefs have on your body, whether you were aware of them or not, and that's okay.

You may have grown up in a family where fertility challenges were not discussed. You may have unexplained anxiety when it comes getting pregnant. Previous family issues were perhaps swept under the carpet, hidden; you learned it was impolite to discuss them. You experienced issues becoming pregnant, so you went to your doctor, who sent you for physical screenings and tests, but your deep-anchored family values or inherited beliefs have not been questioned or screened, up to this point.

Know that you are here now, learning, growing, and evolving. This is the inner work, to uncover, discover, heal, and make this vital shift in mindset. Now you have this blessed opportunity to bring your awareness to those old beliefs, old thoughts, old fears, and old worries that consumed you and turned into self-fulfilling prophecies, generating the negative results you have been experiencing.

You will discover that you have way more power in this situation than you thought. Perhaps you have been unconsciously discounting that notion. If this is making you feel a little vulnerable or uncomfortable, that is great; it means you are already creating space for and allowing this mindset shift to happen. I am here with you. It is safe for you to stay, deal with these feelings, and overcome them. You might want to grab a pen and piece of paper, or open the notes on your phone, and write down all that can be celebrated right now.

Do you have a monthly cycle? Yes? That is something to celebrate; your body is functioning beautifully. Do you have a job or a way of supporting yourself and your child? Yes? That is something to celebrate. Do you have a roof over your head, somewhere for your baby to live safely? Yes? That is something else to celebrate.

Jot down a list of the things that are going well in your life right now, as detailed or as vague as you wish. Write down all the supports you have in place, all the loving people around you, and the great beneficial opportunities you have that you can share with your child. Now notice if jotting this list down brings up happy feelings, or are you judging yourself or feeling ashamed? Are you making up stories to embellish this list? Where does the mind take you? What comes up for you?

Feelings of shame can pop up unexpectedly sometimes. Notice where you feel shame in your body; what does it feel like? Now put an image to that feeling. What does it look like, the first vision, image, or impression? What do you need to do change the image and the sensation? Do you need to break something up, untie something? Perhaps you need to open a door and set it free? Do you need to disperse dark clouds?

Whatever popped up for you, work with it; allow your intuition to guide you. Then change the image. Guilt is also a really common emotion; guilt that you did not do enough, that you are not good enough. These emotions can feel complex. If you feel stuck, be okay with that; this is exactly the right place to help overcome your emotional blockers that have been impeding you on your journey. Trust in the power of this crucial inner work. Look at that paper; what does it represent? Does it represent everything you want to be, do, and have as a parent (a good provider, a loving support system, etc.)?

Another reason you may be experiencing difficulty is because of mixed messages. I often meet clients who desperately want a baby, but they have something on that particular month or a major six-month project in work that is burning in the back of the mind, feeding into the notion that the timing is not right. They pretend they don't care if they are not pregnant that month, yet they are totally devasted when their period arrives. They didn't even want to be pregnant that month or the following.

Their goal was for a totally different month. This flip-flopping over and back, mixed messages, pretending they don't care when they really do, have you found yourself in this exhausting cycle? The desire can be overwhelming when you are scared of wanting it too much. You end up doing a lot of sidestepping around feelings and conversations. This facade, pretence, and denial send out really vague messages and vibrations about what it is you actually want, instead of being really clear. You're afraid of cursing yourself if you say it out loud, often not even sharing this timing/work concern with your partner, feeling added guilt about that too.

Holding it in, suppressing and carrying the brunt of this added guilt, adds to all the other mounted stress. This current situation creates a topsy-turvy roller coaster of emotions. It does not mean anything bad about you as a person; you can be a good person, a great person, a loving person. It can represent an energetic glass ceiling of sorts.

Maybe you are looking at other people right now and feel they are more worthy or deserving than you; this is also impacting your energy and stress levels. Those around may even be contributing to this glass ceiling because of their beliefs or blocks; perhaps a family member, peer, or doctor is constantly referring to your weight or age, or a consultant emphasises low- or poor-quality eggs or sperm. Their judgement or opinion adds to the stress; you take on their blocks as well.

There are a lot of hidden reasons why you feel stuck and stagnant on your journey. I know this feels really real to you right now. I promise, addressing these blocks from multiple angles will be really inspiring, with many aha moments along the way to you becoming and feeling empowered.

If you are feeling frustrated about where you are at right now, this is a sign that you are ready to move on, heal up, let go, and receive your desire. Connect the dots to where you are right now and the memories that surfaced in the previous chapter, your past family lineage. How does this relate back to your family motto? You may be stuck at a very significant place for your family; for example, you may have a thriving business or have been promoted to a high level in work that you have no intention of giving up; perhaps your mother had to give up work to have you.

You may have to unravel feelings about that; on some level, you may be resisting this, as it seems disrespectful to your mother. Maybe you had a sibling who screamed at you as a child, saying something like, "You are very bossy; I would hate for you to be my mother," or the idea of stretching to juggle both a stressful job and a baby may seem extremely tiresome. You may doubt having enough energy for both? Or you may secretly worry your friends will not have time for you anymore. What is coming up for you?

Let us acknowledge this, because the fear of rejection or the fear of being shunned from your family or community is very real and plays a big part in the background. In years gone by, there would have been serious consequences. Now, in this day and age, it is not uncommon to go against your family or society, but it may still feel scary on the inside, with fears and worries lurking in the corners of your mind. That might explain a lot about why you may be holding yourself back. If you discover that one of your hidden family values is resilience ("There is no easy way to have a baby"), then maybe you subconsciously make things harder for yourself to prove that you are worthy of fitting in.

You may have a subconscious belief that getting pregnant easily would show that you are not resilient enough. If pregnancy happens too easily to you when others around you have struggled and suffered, it may not feel fair on some level. If things seem easy, perhaps your period was a day or two late, you unknowingly sabotage it, procrastinate, flip-flop back and forth with worries and excuses: "I don't want to be pregnant this month" for whatever excuse pops up, or you outright reject pregnancy.

Remember, my family motto and what I grew up listening to was, "It's nice to be important, but it's more important to be nice. There's no easy was to have a baby. You were my smallest baby and my biggest ouch." Those limitations are very subtle, yet very real. Take that last one; I constantly heard this on repeat, even though my mother was joking about it and did not mean anything by it. Can you imagine having transference? I not only saw the pain on her face whenever she said the phrase, I also felt it. Not only that, I prided myself on helping people, but I was subconsciously aware that I was my mother's greatest pain. I had to unravel that fact. Perhaps for you it was "It's nice to be important, but it's more important to be nice"; if "nice" is your unspoken family value and you hold a particularly important career role that you have no intention of giving up, then that may evoke inner turmoil of wanting both but subconsciously feeling you have to choose or sacrifice.

Subtle limitations, yet very real.

Our next exercise will shed some light on what your capacity is to receive. Are your body and mind aligned for pregnancy right now?

Think of your ability to receive a child into your life right now; now put an image on that. Imagine it was a symbolic container or something that symbolises what you are allowed to receive; it can be any size or shape. It is fascinating to see what surfaces; what does it look like? What's the first vision, image, or impression that pops up? Visualise its shape. It will give you another angle and clue to uncovering your subconscious blocks. So just take a moment and see what appears in front of you right now. Have a look at its size, texture, and shape. It could be a physical container or something that is quite symbolic. Just see what pops up. Maybe your container is exceedingly small; maybe it is the size of a football stadium, but the roof is on, which means nothing can flow in if the roof is closed.

So with that image in mind, work on opening it; remove the lid, change the image in whatever way, so circumstances and opportunities can flow into your container with ease. Imagine lying down on the grass in the football stadium, pressing a button, and the roof opened so the sunshine poured in, along with the abundance of joy, happiness, and opportunities having a baby in your life will bring. You'll easily receive more and more joy, happiness, fun, laughter, and family togetherness.

What is your present container for abundance? Is it something that represents not only your current limiting situation but also your capacity to receive in the future? Maybe your container is like a rusty old bucket with a hole in it, so not only is your container uninspiring, but your abundance runs straight out as fast as it comes in. Maybe it's something tiny and precious, but there is just no room to take in more.

As you think about the shape, also think about the material and pattern design. As you hold it, see what you see, feel how you feel, hear what you hear. Think about the symbolism of it. What does it say about you? What does it say about your current limitations? What does it say about your current ability to expand? Are you surprised by what came up? Are you surprised by the different answers you received?

This is the power of opening up to the possibility to allow this into your life; you don't have to wait to be perfect. You don't have to wait for an exact thing to happen first. You can simply accept where you are right now; allow this to come to you, and receive it graciously, with open hands, rather than hunting it down and seeking it out.

Small yet profound and powerful shifts of the mindset can make all the difference in becoming pregnant this very month. That is the power of this work. It may take a little reconditioning to release those generational habits and stories so you can create a new normal for yourself; connecting the dots between your past experiences and your current situation is a really powerful start, but working with the visualisation of your container and redesigning it entirely, so it works for you and your future, will result in an even greater shift.

Even if you think you cannot visualise, think again, and begin by working with your other senses. Maybe you hear the sound of your container, like a creaky old door that gets stuck ajar when you open it. Perhaps your sense of smell is the strongest sensory organ;

work with that. What does the container smell like? Is it stinky and gone off? How would you like to change it? What does it need to smell like to be appealing? The more you can incorporate the senses, the faster your outcome will be.

Have fun here; look at the container through the eyes of a child filled with curiosity, wonder, and awe. Bring in excitement, joy, laughter, smiles, cuddles, fun family times.

Having a baby is supposed to be a joyous, happy time. Choose to make it so, and declare out loud to the universe that you are ready to receive. I promise you, the universe will send you opportunities to receive over the next few days; it may come in the form of a compliment. Instead of rejecting it, say, "Thank you."

Make sure to acknowledge that you received the compliment. If a friend offers to buy you coffee, say, "Yes, please; thank you very much." Whatever kindness you are offered, be sure to accept it graciously. It is going to start a chain reaction of receiving abundance, receiving things into your life that you are grateful for.

The more you are grateful, the more you will receive to be grateful for. You will reinforce your new inner knowingness that you can be a parent and actually enjoy it. Even though you will not have all the answers, you know that there is no challenge you cannot overcome. You can experience abundance of joy and happiness. You will receive more awareness to more shifts and thoughts that can be changed. Practice working with your container; visualise it growing to your optimal level so more abundance and fun times can flow into your life. Practice receiving with gratitude.

Trust this work; I have consulted with people from all backgrounds, circumstances, and professions, all relationship types, and real genuine people just like you. You've got this. You can forgive yourself for mistakes of the past, yours and your family lineage, and move on, because this is important.

It is important for you to experience all you desire. You can be a parent; people who look like you can be parents. Same-sex couples can be parents; even teachers and forty-year-olds can be parents. There are no limits anymore about who can become parents. Understanding this will mean the world will shift in more positive ways for you now.

You are ready, even if you think you are not ready yet, thinking, *I'll just lose some weight, I'll get more organised, I'll wait until XYZ are in place.* No, the future will not change unless you make changes now. Even if your present reality has no role models of a work-life balance, you can be the role model for yourself, and the ripple effect of that will be huge.

Becoming aware of your patterns is most of the work. Awareness and change are brought about by applying the supportive techniques in this book so you don't backslide into old sabotaging habits. Now is the moment of power, and all power comes from within. You are ready. Soon, your goals and desires will come willingly and joyfully to you. Magical things happen, not by magic but by design; they happen when you declare confidently, out loud, with deep feeling and meaning, that you are ready: "I am ready to receive."

It is your time. You are ready for the next step. Allow this work to percolate. Notice what manifests for you. It really is your time, and you are truly ready for the next step.

Befriending Your Period

The Most Dreaded Time of the Month

Over and over, clients are extremely positive for the first three weeks of their cycle, but then comes the dreaded period week; the mere thought of it can bring up so much fear (It's never going to happen), worry (When will it happen?), anxiety (looking and watching out for their period every time they use the bathroom, beating themselves up with negative self-talk, followed by an influx of feelings of anger, frustration, even hatred of their body). Have you found yourself in this trap?

This is totally understandable; it is so hard to have your hopes repeatedly dashed. I get it, but if you are constantly looking for and waiting for your period to arrive, guess what? It will.

Energy flows where attention goes; what you send out, you get back. If you are putting your focus and awareness on the dread of your period's arrival, you are essentially putting your focus, energy, and attention on your period. Your body interprets that focus as a command to give you your period, thinking you want it to arrive; so what is the opposite? Change your thoughts, and change your world.

Instead of labelling this dreaded week as "your period week," you could rename it to your "positive pregnancy week," "your test week," or whatever other expression feels right for you that places your focus, awareness, attention, and energy on what it is you actually wish to experience. How would that change things? How easier would it be to go to the restroom if this intention were strongly in place?

Applying and implementing that shift has generated positive results for many beautiful clients, and it can for you too; imagine sharing your fabulous news with your partner now. By completely changing the dread of your "period week" to embracing, trusting, and believing in your "positive test week," you too can experience the elation of discovering you are pregnant.

Remember, if you expect to get your period, you will. It does not matter that you do not want it to come. Whatever your energy and thoughts are focused upon, that is what will manifest. I know it is easier said than done, but I promise if you can shift your thoughts, you will create a great energetic shift that will bring the positive results you deserve.

I suggest you go as far as putting a picture of a positive pregnancy test on the inside of your bathroom door, as a constant reminder to focus on what it is you actually want, instead of living in fear, worry, and dread. This simply shift will make a profound difference.

Firstly, you must befriend your period; please make peace with it now. Thank your monthly cycle and your beautiful body. Please thank your period, even if you do not currently have a cycle, or it is irregular. This gratitude alone is enough to get your cycle back on track. Think about all the confusing messages your body has been receiving; comprehend the inner turmoil that has been going on. Your body did not know if it was coming or going; see the clarity in all the mixed messages. Bring your body, mind, and emotions onto the same page, so they are all working in unison, instead of fighting against each other.

It is okay if your period comes this month. Thank it, as without your cycle, nothing would happen at all. Your body is your friend; it needs you to nurture and appreciate it so it can lovingly hold, nurture, and carry your precious baby. You must work together with your body.

Entertain this idea in order to begin shifting your energy from needy desperation and disappointment to lovingly understanding and allowing a positive test to show up. Focus on what you would love to see happening; see yourself jumping for joy, holding your positive pregnancy test in your hands, versus what you are scared will happen: the arrival of your period. If it does show up, simply thank it, and be kind to yourself; invite this period to be a cleansing period where you release old emotions, old worries that are held and stored in your womb. Remember, we carry our emotions in our womb; see this period as an opportunity to have a great big clear-out in preparation for your baby's arrival.

Fertility Simplified

Let us break down fertility into the simplest understanding possible. As humans, we want to love and be loved. Especially babies; they love to be loved. Love brings joy, happiness, and well-being, evoking wonderful feelings and sensations in your body, mind, heart.

Your body will always want to move towards pleasure, joy, and happiness—because it feels good. Your body will always want to move away from pain, hurt, and upset—because it feels bad.

That is an extremely simplistic revelation, yet it can take active work and determination to implement.

When you are longing for a baby, particularly after a long time, you think you will be happy when you have your baby, but in reality, you are feeling bad and upset due to pregnancy not happening yet. Weeks turn into months. Months turn into years. Every time you hear someone else's news, or your period arrives, the actual feelings being experienced and felt in your body are that of pain, loss, hurt, upset, rejection, and fear. Would you agree?

If this same emotional cycle plays out over and over, which it does, looping in your mind like a hamster wheel running really, really fast, your body associates *baby* with pain and not with the happiness you think. Pain—your body wants to avoid, instead of the joy it would gladly welcome.

Think of all the scenarios: the mere sight of your period arriving, the feeling of your period about to start, the pain and emotional roller coaster of another failed round of IUI/IVF, a friend or relative sharing their good news (even though you are happy for your friend or relative).

Stronger undercurrents of emotions and feelings flow through your body: pain, loss, rejection, hurt, and jealousy, even followed by upsetting thoughts: *When will it be my turn? Why can't I get pregnant?* That keeps the hamster wheel spinning, sparking even more feelings of pain, loss, hurt, upset, along with those sinking, dreaded, twisted, knotted, tensing, tightening, heavy sensations in your chest, stomach, or head.

There is a lot going on inside you on many levels, physically, mentally, emotionally, when you think you are happy for the other person. Take a moment now to recall how you truly felt the last time you heard someone else's news; be completely honest with yourself here. What feelings, thoughts, or emotions arose? What exactly came up for you? This cycle has to be changed from upset to celebration; you must feel joy and happiness first so your body can rewire and associate *baby* with *joy* instead of with *upset*.

Emotions will always win out, especially if the stronger emotions being felt start to entwine and web in associated with *baby*. Your body listens to your fears. It will protect you from them by steering away from pain, loss, hurt, upset, rejection, feeling bad, or becoming pregnant—because it does not feel good or safe to do so. The body has this outstanding ability to memorise, to move towards pleasure because it feels good and away from pain because it feels bad.

Love is warmth, connection, and feeling good; fear, however, creates a separation, feelings of unworthiness, being afraid of rejection. Energy flows where attention goes; this is a powerful concept when used in the correct way. It will allow you to step out of that hamster wheel and break the mundane cycle keeping you in this rut of feeling powerless.

Now is the moment of power. Allow the veil to be lifted so this pattern's clarity can be witnessed. Work with motivation, moving yourself towards trust and a new-found belief. Steer yourself away from fear and pain. What we fear most in life is any kind of rejection. Even the thought of a potential rejection is enough to create stress and tension in your body. "What if time is running out? What if my eggs are too old? What if they don't like me and I'm not good enough?" All these "What ifs," like "What it if doesn't happen?"

Then think again, *What if it does happen?* Begin by changing your thoughts, and notice how your body responds to your new thoughts. How does that different thought feel? Your mind will bring up all this distraction of potential rejection, which plays havoc and causes chaos in your life. Acknowledge this looping inner turmoil. You have the power to change it.

How do you get out of this loop? Constantly bring your mind back into the present moment, back to *What if it does happen?* Invite that mindset shift to filter into the cells of your being, opening up to the possibility and allowing your body to feel safe and happy, so it can happen.

The barrage of the mind filled with doubt has formed a habit of not believing. Every time you trip yourself up with a negative, doubting thought, simply catch yourself and bring yourself back on track by changing your thoughts. Right now, in this present moment, the past cannot hurt you unless you go there; as long as you are here in this moment, you are not there. You cannot get wet by yesterday's rain, and you cannot get burnt by tomorrow's sun. Here in this present moment is where life is. This is where your power is. This is where your trust and belief need to be.

Memories of unhappiness of the past can be projected onto the future, but what you are doing is playing with your imagination because none of that exists in the here-and-now. What you can do here is trust: *I can get pregnant.* The more you keep your focus here in the now, the easier it is, the more joyous it is, and the quicker this will happen for you. It takes an act of will to purposely take yourself out of distraction, out of past upset or future anxiety and back into this present moment of trust. The fastest way to enhance your trust is to visualise your pregnancy vividly, incorporating all your senses.

Imagine you are pregnant right now. What does it feel like to be pregnant? See yourself pregnant. How does it taste? What does it smell like? Listen to the sounds of pregnancy. Do not think of anything until you have sensory awareness in the present moment, which will calm your emotions, mind, and body. When you feel good, then work on your plan; see it, feel it, believe it. Use positive affirmations; if the mind wanders into the past or the "don't wants," then just bring it back into the here-and-now of this present moment, reaffirming "This is happening. I am actively working on taking back my power. All power comes from within. We are creating our baby."

Open up to the limitless field of possibilities within your own body-mind sensory system, activating high levels of creativity, intelligence, and innate wisdom within. We have to begin by letting go of old structures, old beliefs, and old habits to acquire new, confident patterns and beliefs. Change your focus. Gather your capacity to accept and manifest the vision of your future, the future that has been waiting for you all your life to show up.

Reconnect with that lure of becoming a parent, that trusted belief within you. When you connect with, access, and envelop that new sense of possibility that is already within you, everything changes, and magic happens. Take an artful approach to achieving your future, encompassing your senses and body-mind-heart connections. If you can see it vividly in your mind's eye and feel it in your heart, you can experience it in this lifetime.

Igniting the senses is important to enhance your deeper discovery. There is so much more to you, and you have far greater power in this situation than you may think. Whatever you have focused on is what you have experienced in life so far; the problem is, we tend to focus on what we don't want rather than on what we do want. Now imagine shifting that focus from what you do not want to what it is you actually do want.

Allow yourself to heal. When you heal, you recover from powerlessness and feel able to take charge of your own life, with a strong new-found trust and belief. Let us begin to ignite all the senses for an expanded use of your body-mind-heart connection and its potential, with high levels of sustained creativity. Become an archaeologist of your own mind; explore and discover what lies beneath.

Have fun actively creating your future by means of your inner sensory capacity for transformation. Now think about something you would really like: to become pregnant, radiant and glowing throughout your pregnancy, pregnant in the next month or two. Hold that strong visualisation in your mind. Now let us use your inward imagery and senses to activate your desired goal. Thinking in images creates fire in the mind, visions in the soul, palpable feelings in the heart, and energy in the body—all helping to accomplish your desired outcome.

Taste: Imagine tasting a crisp juicy apple; now imagine tasting vanilla ice cream. Now taste hot buttered toast; imagine tasting a healthy salad with a little bite to it. Taste a cake topped with dark chocolate and whipped cream. Now taste something from the celebratory dinner you are going to have on accomplishing your goal: a positive pregnancy test.

Smell: Smell something associated with your desired goal: a garden of roses, the ocean waves as they lap against the shore, a meadow after a rainfall, hot popcorn, a pine forest, bread baking, the scent of a newborn baby.

Sight: See a glorious sunrise, see a magnificent colourful sunset, see a space shuttle taking off in 5, 4, 3, 2, 1, lift-off, see a shooting star in the night sky, see the face of someone you love and adore, see your own face, see your completed goal, see yourself holding your baby in your arms; look down and stare directly into her or his eyes.

Touch: Touch and rub the soft fur of a puppy, plunge your hands into a barrel of crisps and break up as many as you can, walk through a swimming pool filled with warm water, play pattycake with a small child, climb a tree, now touch your goal: have a sense of touching your baby bump, planting soothing kisses on your baby's forehead, gently rubbing the side of his or her cheek.

Hearing: Hear the rain falling on a roof, hear an opera singer holding her highest notes, hear the eruption of applause, hear a group of children playing in the playground, listen to the sound of laughter, hear Dr. Martin Luther King Jr. giving his "I Have a Dream" speech, hear something that has to do with the accomplishments of your goal, hear the gurgling sounds of your baby as she or he lays contently in the crib.

Taste, smell, see, touch, hear, and feel your desired goal again; run it through all your senses again to engage the power of your subconscious mind, your hormonal energiser, boosting your I can, I will, I am. Think and act in imagery. Enrich your concepts and ideas; lay down your foundations and pathways to appreciate the world around you and within you.

Ignite new-found trust and belief. This is it; pregnancy is happening. You can feel it in the core of your being. Incarnate your goal. See it manifested; feel what that feels like, and do a "We did it" happy dance. See it take up residency in your body, mind, heart, and enhance your energy with an abundance of inner passion of achievement. Become more acute and aware, seeing, feeling, hearing things in new ways. Broaden your horizon and expand your perspective.

You're feeling more capable of solving problems in ways that perhaps seem quite magical and even miraculous. Use your body-mind connection in positive ways; see through the perspective of who you really are and what your incredible body is capable of. Step out of your own way by simply allowing your goal to be a part of your life. Know you are worthy to receive and experience it. The positive way of looking at life is a complex yet simplistic dance of shifting awareness. Connect to the greater story beneath; meet yourself at the level of deep listening. When stories beneath are shared and heard, you forge a new understanding and pathway.

When we see ourselves through distorted lenses, labels, and stereotypes, we are in relationship with our expectations and not our true abilities. Stories open the window of direct perception; a great story can fill you with passion for the possible and give you access codes to infinite outcomes.

You are a great story, one of the ultimate Olympic champions, one of the millions of sperm that made their way upstream against the insurmountable odds and came together with its cosmic other half to fuse gloriously in an explosion of new life, so don't think you've never accomplished anything. You are miraculous.

Strip away empty hopes; dreams often seem like a kind of myth, but what happens in a myth is that the suffering comes in the middle of the story; at the end of the story, growth and understanding are found, a resurrection, a rebirth into new ways of being. Cross the threshold from old worn-out beliefs, including holding yourself back, and step into new adventures, new challenges, new learnings.

Your essential self has a radiance that your usual self does not; it is in touch with your life and true meaning, the wisdom of your heart and the earth. It can put you in touch with the unexplored capabilities of your mind and body. It knows the maps of your soul and the treasures that can be found within. Feel it; be touched by it. It is calling you forth with love, encouraging you, empowering you, cherishing you with such deep appreciation for who and what you are. See yourself in fulfilment of your creative genius. It knows why you are here, what you can do, where you can go, and why you need to go there. It is your essential self, your mysterious self, who is always there, no matter how much you have denied its existence. It is there for you, your great friend within. Open your aspiration to the longing intention of your soul. Align your body, mind, heart.

Awaken to your life's purpose; what you do and do not do make a profound difference; feel this yearning, and raise the bar on who you are. Develop a passion for the possible; why do I yearn for this so much, when it is not happening? It is time now for new ways of doing, seeing, and being.

Become your own artist of your destiny, co-designing and co-creating your future. Learn ways to enhance your own physical body through the senses, such as physical activity and savouring healthy meals; through imagery of discovery, seek out your own hidden blocks and messages. As you work with these methods, you will gain an enormous infusion of passion and possibility.

What you once thought impossible will now feel absolutely attainable. You're reinventing yourself; using imagery in a different way, see your body working at its optimal level, healthy, filled with vitality and well-being. You're building a new blueprint, a new way of being, with endless possibilities in your life. Learn to think in images. You have within you a limitless field of intelligence. You can grow exponentially in all aspects of your life. You are unstoppable. Reframe your life, turning your blocks and challenges into inner strengths.

Unleash your joy, and become abundantly radiant. Approach things with a learner's mindset: What can I learn? How can I grow? Celebrate the desire of possibilities before they come into your reality. Embody a celebratory mindset. Discover what the possible is.

I can. I will. I am.

Lifestyle Factors

Outside Influences That Affect Conception

Career

It is so important to give attention to these next issues. Let's face it; if you work full time, you spend more time there, with your work colleagues, than you do with your family and loved ones. So whatever job you choose to do, it must bring you an element of joy and happiness. Sometimes in life, we find ourselves in habitual situations and feel we have to do it, such as "I have to go to work to pay the bills," but how happy does your current career choice make you feel? Is it just a job that brings you more misery than joy?

Do you have an overwhelming job, where you feel you cannot say no or do not want to let people down, so you end up going in early, staying late, and taking on extra responsibility?

> Do you have a stressful job?
> Where do you feel the effects of your job in your body?
> What does it feel like?
> Is it a knotted, twisted, or sharp sensation?
> Put an image to it; what does it look like?
> What is the very first vision or image that arises?
> Stay with that image. Stay with that place in your body; your intuition will guide you.
> Change the image and feel the physical sensation change also.
> Well done; take in a big, beautiful breath, and exhale fully, all the way out.

Perhaps you feel, *I'm not where I want to be or thought I would be in my career yet*, and subconsciously you always thought, *I would be doing XYZ by the time I have a baby.* Have you recently started

87

your own business and feel you must tend to it like a baby? Are there ongoing issues with work colleagues or your boss that are stressful right now? Are your conversations outside of work consumed by what is going on in work? Is your current job stressing you out to the point where it keeps you awake at night?

High stress levels from your working environment may be the very reason you are not getting pregnant; you may think it will be fine when you have your baby because you'll be off work then. Please know that approach will not work. This stressful, upsetting situation needs to be acknowledged and addressed now.

All of this stress brings on rapid breathing, sleepless nights, and tension, which trigger your body into fight-or-flight mode; remember, when your body goes into fight-or-flight mode, as a way of protecting you and keeping you safe, the very first system to shut down is your reproductive system (this vital system needs to be healthy and well when wanting to conceive). High stress, worry, and anxiety also weaken your immune system and zap your energy, joy, and happiness.

Imagine you were a silent witness; look in on your work environment now from the outside. Look at all the people stressing you out in your current working conditions. What changes need to be implemented? Is this the right environment to be pregnant in? Are you surrounded by positivity or negativity? Is this an unfriendly, counterproductive environment? Is there constant toxic gossiping going on, either in the background (you think it has no impact on you) or something you actively engage in?

When you tune into your body and think of work, what happens? What part of your body tightens, tenses, or constricts? Does your body feel like a pressure cooker waiting to explode or a volcano waiting to erupt?

Notice where this work anxiety shows up in your body; it may be in your stomach, chest, or your shoulders. On a scale of zero to ten, how intense does that anxiety feel? More than you thought, no doubt. It is imperative to acknowledge how you feel, to view work like an outsider looking in, and to see things with a whole new perspective. See what you see, feel how you feel, hear what you hear. Is there a solution or resolution to what is going on? Are you open to the possibility of exploring another workplace or job? Here is a big one: Can you change your thoughts to change your own work environment and experience? Can you choose to focus on what is going well, rather than what is not going so well?

Can you choose to take back your own power right now in this moment and make a conscious decision to take the emphasis off that certain annoying person? Let me share with you the best tool I've ever come across to deal with what may feel like a powerless situation. This powerful technique will help you rise above blame and excuses, the "he said, she said" moments of despair. Nothing good ever comes out of being stuck and stagnant in these back-and-forth situations. All healings come from within; choose now to be the bigger person, rise above the drama, rise above the trauma. See how you can make work more joyous so you can thrive through pregnancy. Gratitude is a phenomenal way to turn things around.

Now imagine and see yourself vividly in your mind's eye, standing tall with your head held high, extending your arm out,, and saying, "They are coming from the best place they know how." That phrase and your stretched-out arm are so profound, it stops the emotions in their tracks from entering your physical body, stops it sitting in on your chest, and unsettling your stomach., This distance creates space, space for a breath, space for understanding, space for compassion, and space for empathy. People are truly coming from the best place they know how. No one knows what is going on in anyone else's life. You cannot control what someone else does or says, but you can control how you react or respond.

By taking back your power, they no longer have the ability to upset you; you are now choosing to keep them and their upsetting words at arm's length. I guarantee you, once you truly take the focus off, everything will change; how people speak to you will change, how people react to you will change, and that positive change is imperative for your health and well-being and achieving your parenthood goals.

You cannot blame your being in this situation on someone else or on circumstances; this profound change must come from you. I know it may feel difficult and challenging, but it is so worth it. Either physically or mentally, stretch out your arm and say, "They are coming from the best place they know how." Feel how good that feels; notice the difference in your body. Think of a current situation at work and repeat again, with arm outstretched, "They are coming from the best place they know how." How empowering and strengthening does that feel in a balanced, non-ego way?

Now, let's take things even further: I want you to imagine that this current situation is happening "for you," and this person was sent on your path for a reason to help you heal something inside. What feelings do they evoke within you? When was the last time you felt that way?

Imagine they are a mirror to help you see inside; this situation is not even about them, but rather to help you grow and learn. What can you learn about yourself? How can you grow and evolve?

This is your new powerful mantra: "May I see clearly the lesson in this to help me grow, and may the situation flow gracefully; may this situation be resolved with love and light."

Homelife

Having a baby is a wonderful, exciting time, yet it can be a little daunting or stressful when you think of all the changes a baby may bring to your life, especially your homelife. Do you currently have space in your home for a baby? Is the spare room your walk-in wardrobe? In the back of your mind, are you wondering where you are going to put all your clothes and shoes?

Are you still in your starter-home and not your forever-home that you would have wished for when having a baby? Think back to when you were a child; what was your dream family house like? Perhaps an idyllic suburban home with a white picket fence, blossoming trees in the garden, a basket of puppies sitting beneath a tree, and children playing happily in the garden, but you are currently living in an apartment on the third floor of a busy building, feeling stuck and feeling like you cannot afford to move.

There's a major mismatch going on in the depths of your mind, because your dream home intention was planted deeply at an early age with such depth, feeling, and meaning. It is like your wedding day; you have an ideal scenario embedded in your subconscious from childhood, right down to the dress.

On some level, your subconscious mind thinks, *Hang on a minute; we're not where we're supposed to be for having a baby. We'll wait until the conditions are right.* Before you think, *Sure, I was only a child then playing,* depending on how convincingly you set that intention, totally unbeknownst to yourself, your subconscious remembers; it took notes like a top student, and now it's acting. Take a moment; get a pen and some paper, and as you begin to scribble, allow that early memory of your ideal scenario to come to mind. Write down or sketch out the important elements. How do you feel about your current dwelling? Do you refer to it as a "house" or a "home"?

Perhaps now is the perfect time to open up to the idea of moving; maybe it's something you've been putting off while prioritising other things, but it needs to be addressed now. Maybe you think moving is not a viable option right now, but perhaps it is. But have you actually taken action to explore the option? This hidden need in the background needs to be acknowledged. The mismatch must come into balance and alignment.

Look at your current home; how can it work for you? Where would you put the crib? Do you need to clear out the cluttered spare room? Will you have to move furniture around to make things work? Begin to see the space changing, flowing, and moving in a better direction for having a baby. If moving is completely out of the question, then settle your mind.

Bring yourself back to childhood; by now, the memory will have surfaced. See yourself playing with your dolls, setting the intention "When I grow up, I'm going to live in this type of house and have X number of babies." Replay the ideal scenario from childhood in your mind, but change the details of the old ideal to your current home's layout; see your house in full detail and describe it, then replay the new ideal in your mind again. Replay it one more time, with as much detail as possible; incorporate all the senses: the smell of your home, the feeling of your home, see yourself touch something in your home, taste something, hear what you hear in your home, and allow these new details to erase the stronghold effect of the old.

Then begin the actual physical process of decluttering in your home, creating space, bringing your vision to life, shifting furniture around if needs be, to get the whole process moving and flowing. Decluttering the whole house, room by room, drawer by drawer, starting one drawer at a time and working your way through, will be such an empowering exercise to do for your body, mind, and soul. Let go of the old, giving away to charity or recycling. Bring new energy into your beautiful home so it no longer feels stuck and stagnant, waiting on the never-never.

Take action to reinforce the subconscious mind that you are ready now; you are in the perfect place to bring your baby home. Visualise clearly coming home from the hospital for the first time with your brand-new baby; see what you see, feel how you feel, hear what you hear, smell what you smell, taste what you taste. Ignite all your senses so you feel, *Yes, this is really happening.*

Family Pressure

The stress family members can put on the couple can be enormous. Parents, well-meaning aunts, brothers, sisters, whoever, joking or not, can have a huge impact and can create a sensational amount of upset, usually totally unbeknownst to the good-willed family member. The minute you walk down the aisle, your wedding day is not even over, and already the barrage of "So when are you having a baby?" starts. Six months pass; bombardment of "Any news yet?" Twelve months goes by; an influx of advice. Two years pass by; "Here's the number of this doctor." Beyond that, the silence.

People mean well and truly want to help, but their help often feels like it comes with judgement or criticism. You meet their well wishes with disapproval; maybe it feels like they are undermining you in some way, but what really happens is the silence, the stares, and the advice are filled with your own expectations or self-doubt.

You expect them to know how you feel, but you don't truly know yourself how you feel. You expect them to know how upsetting their comments are to you, but you don't even know yourself why those things are upsetting you so much. The tug-of-war between bravery and deep upset is just too overwhelming; it is such a sensitive time, and they honestly have no clue how you feel.

You put on a brave face; meanwhile, inside, your body is coiling, tensing, and twisting. Learning to understand what is happening on a cellular level is paramount in handling expectations and unwelcome advice in a graceful way, so you're not left feeling upset or angry at the do-gooder.

> Expectations are strange creatures and have a life of their own, they have the ability to affect how your life plays out. When you use expectations with skill and awareness, they focus your energy to accomplish the great things you strive for; however, when not used correctly, expectations can be one of the greatest forms of self-torture.
>
> —Stewart Blackburn

An expectation is a belief that something in particular is definitely going to happen. In fact, you are so sure of your expectation that you eliminate all doubt of what is coming. That's what makes it so powerful when used correctly but so devastating when not.

When you expect something to happen and it does not, you generally default to disappointment or sadness, but you are the one who created the expectations. They are not laws of nature. Expectations are tools for organising your future; sometimes, you even use expectations retroactively, as in expecting your parents to have done things differently when you were younger, which is a twisted way of wishing things were different and blaming the people who did the best they knew how to, for the things they could not have foreseen.

May I guide you now, to lift yourself out of the realm of blame and excuses; by default, we tend to find ourselves in these places of hurt, upset, and heartache. If you took that silent witness viewpoint here and look in on your situation from afar, what can you see clearly now that you did not notice before?

Gently place your hand on your heart now and ask yourself, "Do I honestly believe my mother [sister, aunt, etc.] wanted to hurt and upset me?" What emotion has come to the surface, waving for your attention? Imagine if that relative was sent on your path for you, to help and guide you, rather than come at you in this situation; what are they reflecting and triggering within you? Some inner fear is reacting to what they said or did; what is it? When was the last time you felt that way? If you shift your perspective here, what can you learn? How can you grow, and how can you evolve?

Relationships

Take an honest-to-goodness look at your relationship now. Relationships can take a lot of hard work, especially during challenging times, and there is nothing more challenging to put a strain on your relationship than longing for a baby, if you allow it. Blame and excuses can seep into the corners of your mind; the biological clock ticking, mixed with the white-knuckle rollercoaster ride of grippy neediness and the strangling control of want. The highs and lows of emotions can really give you a distorted outlook on things.

Be totally honest: Are you in a solid relationship, or do you feel time is running out, and you must have a baby because there is no time left to find a new partner? Be honest: Is this your dream life partner, someone you can see yourself happily with for the rest of your life? Can you accept them for who they are, as they are, bad habits and all?

Do you secretly wish your partner would change, but no matter how much you guide and advise, she or he does not listen or do what you ask? This creates great inner upset and turmoil. Is your relationship consumed by what your partner is not doing right instead of focusing on what they are doing right?

Relationships can also consume your energy and zap your happiness, if you allow it. May I suggest redirecting the awareness and shifting the focus to acknowledge and reinforce what is going well in your relationship; this change is so beneficial and has a joyous ripple effect.

Learn to accept your partner for who he or she is, knowing the only person you can change in this world is you. You can be a wonderful beacon of light, guiding your partner in the right direction, which takes you leading the way, not forcing the change. Recall to mind what attracted you to your partner; what do you love about her or him?

Be that silent witness; look in on your relationship from afar. Can you see ways of enhancing your relationship right now? Can you come together on the same page going forward to achieve your shared goals, hand-in-hand? Can you see situations in your relationship where your energic shield may come in useful? "They are coming from the best place they know how"; maybe it's a place of stupidity, and that is okay. Invite that space of understanding and perhaps a smile to arise too. If you genuinely love your partner and know in your heart and soul you are meant to be together, and having a baby is what you both want, be kind to one another. Let go of the need to find fault; instead, choose to find gratitude and appreciation for all the amazing things he or she does for you. Find ways of rekindling your romance, togetherness, and shared happiness. Kindness and compassion are the only joyful way forward.

It may feel like you have been on this journey a long time, trying everything; the frustration can take hold. One partner's headstrong determination, "This has to work," takes over; perhaps you feel like that, but have you explored the option of your partner's energy holding you back? Are they going along with having a baby and all these IVF procedures to please you? Do they truly want a baby for themselves? What are their fears around having a baby?

They may have unresolved issues to address before you can bring a baby into the world together. Having a baby is a wonderful, exciting time, but it can also be a scary time; old feelings of childhood can resurrect. Feelings of "I'm not good enough" may arise from nowhere.

Set aside time out for each other, creating a safe space for you both to be brutally honest with each other, allowing each other to be heard. Together, acknowledge your fears, no matter how trivial they may seem; they are very real and valid for you both and need to be listened to and heard.

Those inner fears may be having a real impact on you and your partner; it's imperative they are expressed and listened to. Be open and honest, especially about the things you are afraid to voice; there is no fear you cannot overcome. Start by saying, "I know it's scary having a baby; how do you feel?" Allow your partner to be heard fully before jumping in with a response.

Embrace the change you both need to make things better, feel more solid, and grow more connected. Learning to communicate fully takes trust. Being open with each other takes honesty; you must believe you are not going to be ridiculed for what you say. The most rewarding skills you will ever develop in your relationship, trust and honesty, will ensure a united front in your new role of parenting together. No challenge is too big to overcome. Trust, honesty, and integrity are everything in your relationship, with or without a child.

Do you need to have closure on a previous relationship? Perhaps you were married or in a long-term relationship before and planned to have a baby with that person, and for whatever reason, the relationship broke down; at that time, you wholeheartedly made a strong vow with that person, which was energetically deep-rooted and probably still held in place today. Let us find that anchor and draw it up and out. You are not delving into anything here; you are just going back to set yourself free. Take back your power from that embedded command and release your energy from the past to enable it to flow into this present time in your life and manifest what you wish to create now.

Recall to mind when you set your wholehearted commitment of having a baby with someone else. Remember how you felt and how deeply committed you were then; life has taken you on a different path, and that's okay. At that time, you were totally committed to having a baby with that other person; where is that vow or commitment anchored in your body? What does it feel like? Now put an image to it, and begin to change the image in whatever way it is calling you to change it.

Now, allow yourself to pull that anchor up; release any attachments to the past. Vividly change the scenario; give yourself full permission to send loving forgiveness or gratitude to your ex-partner. Thank them, looking back only to see how far you have come, how much you have grown and learned about yourself and your strength. Set yourself free from that past experience; declare yourself free from that past relationship, free from guilt, free from bitterness, free from resentment. Remember, anger and bitterness are like drinking poison yourself and expecting someone else to die. They don't care that you harbour such feelings; they have moved on, and now it is your turn to joyously move on too.

Change the initial inscription of any energetic contract to your current partner's name, choosing this partner to have a baby with; as you do, notice how you feel. Feel the impact of the original deep-rooted intention melting, softening, draining away. Feel the massive weight you did not even know you were carrying, lifted up and off. Feel that new breath of life, that deep inner freedom and liberation.

Extend gratitude to the past; see how far you have come in life. Allow past hurts to melt away to set your future free, being grateful now for the lessons learned and good times shared. Also give yourself permission to let that old hold go completely; it no longer serves you well. Invite your present-day partner into the vision, and for the ultimate healing, release yourself on the deepest level. You can even envision the two partners shaking hands as a sign of mutual respect and blessing to each other to move forward, living your best life on your new path of freedom, joy, and happiness.

Money Worries

Money insecurities create phenomenal feelings of inadequacy and play a huge part in not conceiving, especially in male fertility issues. They instill deep feelings of inadequacy: "How can I provide for my family? I have nothing to give," resulting in the physical conditions of low sperm count, poor motility, or the ultimate condition of azoospermia, where no sperm is produced at all.

Anger, frustration, worries, fears, and anxiety around money and your financial situation are the emotions directly behind sperm issues and persistent lower back pain, having a direct impact on the physicality of wanting to make babies. Those negative emotions zap your energy by depriving your life of meaning and purpose.

Money worries transmute into a harsh belief, thinking you will not be able to pay for the situation you are facing, creating a belief that "babies are expensive." Inner worries leading to sleepless nights are detrimental. The body trips into fight-or-flight mode, preventing the desire you want most from happening.

Being in debt triggers deep emotional responses of denial. Lower back pain is directly caused by money worries and relationship strains. You're trapped in a continuous cycle of pain and discomfort, one feeding the other. Change cannot happen until the true belief around money is recognised. Did you grow up with the belief that "Money doesn't grow on trees. Money is bad, and rich people are mean. Money is the root of all evil"? What is your inner belief around money? What are your partner's inner belief around money? Are you good with money, or does it burn a hole in your pocket?

Allow any and all money concerns to spring to mind. Then ask yourself, are these beliefs true? Are they kind? Are they even valid or worthy? Do these old beliefs stop you in your tracks, hamper your success, and serve no purpose in your life? Transform money worries from distorted beliefs into developing a new relationship with money. You can have money and be a nice person; begin to open up to the possibility of money being good. Can you allow the ebb and flow of giving and receiving money into your life?

The flow of money is supposed to be dynamic; it comes, and it goes. Like the breath, it comes in, it goes out. Like gentle lapping waves, they flow in, they flow out. In Europe, on the back of every euro note, there is a bridge, a big, wide, sturdy open bridge. It's free flowing; it's not a scary little rickety bridge, where you're frightened to take a step for fear of falling through the cracks. Why?

One of the top feng shui masters designed the euro note with this principle of nature in mind: the ebb and flow of giving and receiving. When this dynamic energy is free to circulate, you too are free to allow your creative ideas to circulate rather than being dampened, stuck, or stagnant. The more you cling to money for fear of lack of, the more lack of money you will experience in life, and the more your conception ideas will be strangled and placed on hold.

Develop a habit of saying thank you when you spend money; say thank you when paying your bills. The more you are grateful for your money, the more money will flow into your life, in ways you never even thought of. If paying in euros, turn the notes bridge side up to allow that dynamic flow of money to be unleashed.

I taught this trick to a client, who played bingo that evening and paid for her booklet bridge side up with ease and gratitude, which was a very foreign concept to her. Previously, she had an awful relationship with money and would have consciously been miserly with her money and hated paying for anything. Guess what? She won at bingo, for the first time ever. It was the first time she ever won anything in her life.

Consciously choose to say thank you in your mind, every time you buy something. Gratitude has an immensely powerful effect. Choose right now to simply have a new relationship with money, allowing the ebb and flow to circulate, allowing your creative juices to flow, whether you wish to give birth to a baby or give birth to a book idea, a new plan, or a project. The release of "not feeling worthy enough" is addressed and altered. Smile into the idea of a dynamic movement of energy associated with the flow of money; releasing fears and concerns around money could be the very thing that gets things moving and flowing in the right direction.

Information Overload

STOP

Do you have a list of things to try and apps to follow? Are you consumed by going to appointment after appointment? Are you obsessed with tracking your ovulation and menstrual cycle through apps on your phone? Are you going to this doctor, that doctor, this therapist, that therapist, following every diet, and taking every supplement suggested? Are you going for acupuncture, going to reflexology, going to this class, that class, reading every book and blog recommended, all in order to tick them off some inner list? But are you actually connecting to any of them?

Do you honestly believe in your heart and soul that they are the right options for you? Have you ever even considered that question? Are you doing things for the sake of it, for fear of missing out, or because you think you have to try everything possible? "That's what Jane down the road did, and she's pregnant now." Are you trying to optimise every possibility in a state of frenzy, just ticking them all off your invented list, regardless of how your body feels or responds?

Let's just take in a big breath now, then exhale fully all the way out; allow your breath to slow down. Invite your mind to slow down; all this rushing, racing, wanting, and doing is exhausting. Just allow all the pressure, tension, and worry to lift.

Discover now how you really feel about each and every thing you are trying; one by one, go through them now. Feel into your body for any reactions such as tightening, tensing, knotting, any sensation at all; your body is fascinating. It will let you know if something feels good or if it doesn't feel right for you.

If you sat down and really thought about it, do you feel comfortable and supported by your doctors? Do you feel listened to or heard, or they are dismissive of you? Tune into their language and words that they use; are they positive or negative? Do they home in on your age, weight, or declining eggs, making you feel worse after you leave their practice? Do you believe that diet or those supplements can truly help? Have you felt any difference in your body at all? Do you belief in acupuncture, or do you find it painful and uncomfortable? Do you feel they may as well be sticking the needles in the wall?

Are you depriving yourself of that cup of coffee or the dark chocolate that tastes so delicious, or secretly feeling miserable missing out on that glass of wine you enjoy with your meal? All of this trying, depriving, doing things you don't truly connect with because a friend recommended it, only generates a great deal of distress and confusion in your body, mind, and emotions.

I suggest you ease off the controlling, planning, diets, restrictions, sacrifices, appointments, and micromanaging, and begin to trust in yourself and trust your body. I even suggest deleting those pressurising apps off your phone, and throw away the stress in a box (ovulation sticks). Your body has incredible wisdom; if you allow your intuition to guide you, it will show you. You will know and understand when you are ovulating, what you connect with, and what you are wasting your time on. Just ticking things off your invented list will not give you the positive results you wish, but all the added stress will just push it further away. Perhaps some body issues are arising beneath your radar; do you feel the need to micromanage and control everything? How did you feel when I suggested you delete the apps and throw away the ovulation sticks? Explore this idea; what is coming up for you?

Did sheer panic set in?

If panic set in at the thoughts of deleting the apps or throwing away the ovulation sticks, ask yourself, why? Why don't you trust yourself or your body's innate wisdom? Remember, your ovaries are ovaries for a reason; they know how to release your eggs. If you allow yourself to become in tune with your body, you will even feel that physical release. Your eggs are eggs for a reason; they are not kidneys, they are eggs and know how to fuse with the sperm to form your baby. Your womb has the knowledge and wisdom to nurture, hold, and support your baby's growth and development. Your body is amazing and just needs the opportunity to feel trusted and feel safe enough to conceive.

Hidden Secrets

Through a gentle yet profound approach, we will turn the tsunami of emotions and challenges into growth and gratitude by delicately uncovering hidden wounds within. Something deep inside you is calling; you can sense its immense presence. You are arriving, homeward-bound, home to yourself with kindness, understanding, and compassion.

You're home, to recognise your true beliefs and identify those that have no purpose, other than hindrance. Lately, you may have felt like there was a fortress deep inside, storing hidden secrets, awaiting this moment of liberation. This freeing awareness is what you have been longing for; you're now ready to understand what has really been going on within. You have been torn, feeling different, feeling pain, feeling something held, frozen, or knotted within. Now, feeling safe, you no longer need to be trapped. Allow the answers to come forth; invite the frozen hidden pain, the fear buried deep inside to reveal itself to you. Invite the river of memories to flow, looking back only to see how far you have come. You have come so far. It is time now for those hidden secrets to reveal themselves. It is time now to melt away the stuckness; see that iceberg crack and break away. It is time now to acknowledge your thoughts and emotions around the old paradigms and beliefs, imposed on you from childhood; it is time now to change them. It is time now to evolve yourself into something new; you are ready to step forward in life. Reach your hand out. Open the door. Step into your own power. You have felt torn for as long as you can remember.

This is the sign you have been waiting for.

The very essence of healing is inner power. When you heal, you recover from powerlessness, from dis-ease, from disharmony; once again, you take charge of your life so you can steer your future toward your greatest joy and fulfillment. However, in a world that is full of opinions and judgements, it can be challenging to find which path makes sense for you.

Huna is a Hawaiian word that means "hidden or secret"; this path of self-discovery will guide you to your own revelation, your own aha moments that make sense for you as to why things are currently happening as they are. My goal and desire for you is that you uncover, discover, and heal from your hidden blocks that are impeding your journey to parenthood.

To look within and find where your problems began; what's their source? The inner subconscious portion of your being operates spontaneously, joyfully, and freely: your inner self believes in your self-image, even though you do not always believe in it.

The subconscious portion of your being functions amazingly, despite facing strong opposition or interference by your beliefs. Each person experiences a unique reality, which is different from any other individual's experience. Your reality springs out from your inner landscape of thoughts, feelings, beliefs, emotions, and expectations.

What is a belief? A belief is something you tell yourself over and over until it becomes a reality for you, but it is not the actual reality. It could be outdated information.

Our beliefs are often so limited. If you believe your inner self is working against you, instead of with you or for you, you will dampen its abilities and force it to behave in a certain way because of your beliefs. Your conscious mind is meant to make clear judgements, but false beliefs will cloud its clear vision.

What is an expectation? An expectation is a belief that something is definitely going to happen; you are so sure of your expectations that you eliminate all doubt. Expectations have a life of their own; they have the ability to affect how your life plays out. When you use expectations with skill and awareness, they focus your energy to accomplish your desires, but when used incorrectly, expectations can be one of the greatest forms of self-torture. That is what makes them so powerful when properly used and so devastating when not.

When you expect something to happen, like each month, you expect to become pregnant, and it does not happen, you generally default to disappointment, sadness, and frustration. You set the expectation in your mind, unaware of your inner beliefs, which do not match your expectation. Let us remember, the energy of your emotions is far greater than thoughts; you can think positive until the cows come home, but unless you feel it, nothing will change. Words are just empty words unless the emotion and feelings behind them resonate and vibrate.

Look at it this way: You probably would not leave a television blaring loudly with a war movie playing in your baby's nursery, would you? Not in a million years. Letting go of negativity on all levels in your own life is like turning off that television and removing it from the nursery completely, opting to play a soothing lullaby instead. Creating a soothing, calming sanctuary, peaceful and serene.

While there will be moments of turmoil in your life, you can breathe into your feelings; you can let your tears flow, if that is what is coming up for you. You can still send a message to yourself that everything is going to be okay. This is the nature of life, and you can handle anything that arises. Letting go of doubts and fears is like moving branches off the trail so there is a clear pathway; your desire can freely come to you. You do not need to hunt it down or seek it out. When the conditions are right within—mindset, emotions, and energy all in alignment—they clear the way, removing the overgrowth from your path, and your goal just effortlessly comes to meet you on your path.

Perhaps you can feel into your body; feel how your heart smiles as you warmly invite your baby to meet you on your path and nestle graciously into your life. When they arrive, there will be a sense of not remembering life without them, as if they have always been there.

Even though there may be much to do in your busy life, set aside time to connect with people who bring you joy, who bring a smile to your face, who fill your belly with laughter. After all, a home filled with the sound of laughter is beautiful, isn't it? As you nurture your closest relationships, let go of the little things that steal away your closeness. A home filled with harmony and closeness is beautifully inviting, isn't it?

When each day comes to a close, you might benefit from protecting your sleep, giving your body time to rest and restore. Recharging your energy, by giving your body ample rest, which is a beautiful thing, all this good care will contribute to your own health. Everything that you put into your body, from the food you eat to the thoughts you think and the emotions you feel, is going to surround and affect your baby also; remember, you take your baby everywhere with you when you are pregnant. Create this beautiful, warm, welcoming sanctuary within you now, filled with positivity, joy, and happiness. Your baby is excited to experience this.

Grace and Gratitude

By now, you should be feeling more empowered in the understanding that you really have the power here. You have the power in this situation. You have the power to choose unwaveringly that this is what you want. When I say grace and gratitude, I mean, make a committed decision with elegance and grace, so it just flows into your life. Decide with commitment this is what you want. Decide what you are willing to give up, so it does not feel like a sacrifice to get what you want. Set your mind to it; see it, feel it, believe it.

Fuel this ability to give yourself a command and follow through on it, with gratitude; you already have the knowledge and the power to accomplish this and most anything you want. In the past, because nobody taught you this, you had not developed a clear understanding of how your mindset plays a phenomenal role in your ability to conceive. 95 per cent of this work is mindset; the paradigms of the mind control habitual behaviour, and 5 per cent is down to the physical act of conceiving. It only takes one egg and one sperm, and there are millions of both. Therefore, we frequently do not do what we already know how to do, resulting in confusion and frustration.

Now the veils are lifting, you can see this clearly. Change the paradigm; clear the image in your subconscious from *I can't* to *I can, I will, I am.* See it so vividly, and reject anything else you have been told otherwise; do not leave it in anymore. You hold the power in this situation—not me, not your doctors, not your family, and certainly not your past.

Gracefully control the flow of your thought energy; let it flow freely to positivity and self-assurance. Let it flow freely to you and through you, with a positive mental attitude, allowing it to improve everything connected in your life. Your thoughts are energy; they have frequency. Negative thinking has a really low vibration, only attracting more misery. Positive thinking has a high vibration on the exact same wavelength as your goal, attracting that directly to you. Think positive.

More than anything else, our attitude at the beginning of any task or goal will affect its successful outcome. There is nothing to be gained by being negative; don't waste valuable time by being consumed by or broadcasting personal problems. Radiating the attitude of well-being and the confidence of a person who knows exactly where they are going will propel you so far forward on your journey, you'll need a telescope to look back and see how far you have come.

Do not take my word for it; experience it for yourself. Life is good when you do; you will find good things will begin happening for you, and fast.

Smile, radiate, and exude that confidence.

Here's an example from one of my clients:

> Hi Jenny,
>
> I can never thank you enough for what you have done for me over the last few months.
>
> I have gone from being introverted, stressed, anxious, and doubting my abilities as a mother to this confident, happy, energetic, vibrant being, oozing confidence in myself. I feel like the world is my oyster; anything I want I can have.
>
> The breathing exercises really helped to relieve stress, and I will be continuing with them daily. The meditations are just amazing; I love the energy and the confidence they give me.
>
> The meditations that I did with you were my favourite; the visions you help me to build, from the wonderful womb and dancing with my eggs to the final one,

where I was walking out of the hospital with my husband and baby, are so clear and vivid, I only have to close my eyes, and I can see everything so clearly.

All the blockages you helped me with have been removed. I no longer have any weight on my shoulders, no sick feeling in my tummy; nothing is weighing me down, and I feel as light as a feather, like I have no problems in the world. Every day, I sing my happy song and dance my happy dance, and I am so grateful for this wonderful life I have been given and the wonderful life I am going to have with my own husband and baby.

I don't think I will ever be able to put into words how amazing this journey has been so far; instead of fixing my problems, I fix my thinking, and then any problems will resolve themselves. You have provided me with this skill, which I will use for the rest of my life, and I am so grateful to have learnt this from you.

I cannot wait to send you a picture of my first scan and work with you on the rest of my pregnancy journey. I have started work on my vision board, and I am so excited to see it when it all comes together.

Thank you so much for everything.

xxxxx

Light-Switch Moment

By changing your thoughts and beliefs, you have the power to change your reality, to change your body, to change your future. That power is immense; this message should permeate deeply in your mind and reverberate now. Choose to love and accept yourself for who you are, as you are; choose to let go of fear. Ultimately, choose to trust and believe in yourself.

Experience a revolutionary overhaul of your thoughts happening and taking place now, creating your fundamental reality. How you experience your emotions can inhibit you from seeing how things really are.

Imagine your beautiful womb and the wonderful space you have created; imagine the nursery in your home with a built-in sound system. See your baby lying in the crib; now think of stress, worry, and tension as a war movie plays with the volume on full blast. Feel the jolts as those noisy, irritating, unnerving sounds pierce your ears. I'm guessing you probably wouldn't play that through the sound system in the nursery; you'd choose a soothing, comforting lullaby instead, right? Yet your negative tensing fears will have a similar effect on your baby, creating distress.

Thoughts can be filled with positive power to expand your view of what is possible.

Disentangle from the frustration, the resentment, the chasing, the wanting, the gripping; it is exhausting. Simply commit to allow your journey to unfold in the light of joy and trust. Open your hands; release the burden.

Let go of any and all attachments to the desired outcome; take a step back, and breathe in deeply. Create space for a whole new perspective, a whole new dimension of enjoyment. Be open to the possibility and reality; this is happening.

Harmonise yourself with comforting, nurturing thoughts that are kind to you, your body, and especially your baby.

The veil that cast a shadow on your awareness is lifting. The things that were once invisible to you are becoming clearly visible, joyous, and beautiful.

Pregnancy is natural and imminent. It is available to you; anything and everything is possible. Trust and gratitude take you out of a place of fear into one of love, out of seeing problems and into seeing possibilities, opportunities, solutions. There is always a way.

See gratitude and blessing in every moment, day, and week. What if there wasn't really a problem, just an old inherited anchored belief? What if that belief was really only a thought that can always be broken down and changed? Does that feel more manageable? Can you begin to see your situation transforming?

What if, as soon as you identified that inherited imprint, opinion, thought, or belief, you instantly changed it? Becoming pregnant would be imminent; would you be willing to make that change? As easy as walking into a room and flicking on the light switch; that's how fast and easy things can and do happen. Once you find the trigger and flick the switch, things will instantly change and happen for you. Your dreams will be forthcoming.

Does it feel empowering to realise your thoughts, beliefs, and perceptions can strengthen and bring to fruition your desires and positive results?

You have the power to identify and influence change.

Dive deeper. Surrender to change; allow that one anchored, entangled thought to become known; all the other thoughts are knotted to it. The hidden one is currently creating your dreaded fears instead of manifesting your true desires.

Open your mind like a parachute. Open your eyes, and lift your gaze to seeing a vast horizon. Open your ears to hearing the gentle whispers of your intuition. Expand your awareness, and feel what is possible.

What is your revaluating stronghold, that aha realisation leading to your own light-switch moment?

Your subconscious knows that answer; not your doctor, not your acupuncturist, not your nutritionist, not your personal trainer, not your friend, not your family, not some well-wisher. You do. You have the answer within you; it's that fear, that thought you are afraid to say out loud. Ask what it is.

I promise you, when you say it out loud, it will not be half as daunting as you envisioned. Say it; what aha, light-switch moment is your intuition revealing and guiding you to? Something will change; something will start moving, shifting, and flowing.

Dissolve the old code of limited nonsense, opinion, or belief down—feel it draining away, all the way away from you.

Now, what if pregnancy could indeed happen this month, which it can? How amazing would that feel? Miracles, even medical miracles, happen every single day.

May today be your day.

Trust yourself completely to discover and experience your pregnancy in delightful and surprising ways. Encourage yourself; be conscious. Something big is happening in the background, even if you are not directly aware of it just yet.

Willingly choose to allow the light to illuminate your heart, your soul, and this great blessing. Now, smile into the idea; feel yourself softening, clearing away those coiled or restricted energy blocks. Joy and happiness are flowing freely.

> You've always had the power, my dear, you just needed
> to learn it for yourself.
> —Glinda, *The Wizard of Oz*

A new freedom, a new beginning awaits you, now that you released the pressurised stronghold; take that long awaited breath in and sigh of relief out. Be willing to let go of your clutched life plan to allow a better, more relaxed plan to unfold. Feel your shoulders; the pressure and responsibility have been lifted off. What does that feel like?

Step forward into a new relaxed role, trusting and believing in the process of life.

Do you have a cat or dog? Have you ever picked them up for a great big cuddle, drawn them close, hugged and squeezed them because you love them so much and needed that cuddle so bad, only to discover all they want to do is run away from you?

But then, when you least expect it, they climb onto your lap and give you the best snuggle ever. If you don't have a pet, think of Elmyra in *Tiny Toons*: "I want to take you home to hug you and squeeze you and kiss you and love you forever."

Elmyra is obsessed—oblivious to her overenthusiastic stronghold of affection (a stranglehold, in her case). She chases them, hunts them down, and traps them to love and baby them, killing them with kindness, squeezing them so tight that all they want is to escape. She's unaware of the negative impact of her behaviour.

Your obsession, like Elmyra's, repelled your pregnancy from you; at heart, she is a sweet girl with an abundance of love to give. You have an abundance of love to give, and by setting yourself free, your baby will come freely to you, just as your dog or cat freely jumped up onto your lap for the best cuddle ever, when you least expected it.

The universe will figure out a way for you. Trust it, and believe it. Know it, and feel it. If you can see it in your mind's eye and feel it in your heart, you can experience it in this lifetime. You have abundance to give; you have so much love and a beautiful home to share. Trust and believe in the process of life, trusting wholeheartedly in your self-worth; you were always worthy to receive.

Now with your light-switch, aha, enlightening moment, knowing it was just an old belief that interfered; your circumstances and your inherited genes do not control your life. You do.

Be inspired. Be empowered to actively create through positive thinking the bright, happy future you wish and deserve to love and behold.

Smile. Be free, and feel the feelings of happiness now; no more waiting. Now is the time for joy and happiness.

Part 3

Taking Back Your Power

Fertility Future

The Spiritual Self

Self-Love, Self-Trust, Self-Worth, and How You Speak to Yourself

"Do you have children?"

A silence follows that dreaded question, a shallow breath, heart-sinking, gut-wrenching, tightening silence. The barrage of internal emotions and negative self-talk can be fundamentally detrimental for your body, mind, and soul.

There's a lot of emotion in that one blink of an eye moment, especially after experiencing a miscarriage or trying everything for years. Not only is that moment filled with your own heaviness of shame, self-doubt, guilt, and uselessness, but the other person's fears and judgements also pour into the mix.

You want the ground to open up and swallow you. You want to run, but you can't. Numbing by distraction is good, as you struggle for a cover-up response.

We are conditioned to habitually ask, "So when are you guys having children?" as soon as someone walks down the aisle. "Do you have kids?" is often one of the first question asked upon meeting someone new. Your only options seem to be run away or numb yourself by distraction, but imagine the sigh of relief you would have if you did not have to squirm, want to run away, or hide your bubbling emotions anymore when asked if you had children.

How beneficial would it be to learn how to stay with yourself and those tightening feelings for a moment, just enough to allow them to be identified and, most importantly, changed. Our self-image—self-love, self-worth, self-trust—is all encompassing; self-image is key to your personality and behaviour. Change your inner self-image and how you speak to yourself, and you will change your personality roadblocks and behaviours. Those intense sensations forming inside are awful and debilitating. Let us work with this scenario now.

Recall to mind that dreaded moment. Notice the exact feeling in that moment. What does that sensation feel like, as opposed to thinking or labeling the emotion? What does it feel like? Where are you feeling it in your body? Now, what does it look like? Put an image to it; what is the very first vision, image, or impression you get? Don't worry how strange or random it may seem. Now what does the image need in order to change it? Your intuition will guide you. Fill the image with positivity and strength, knowing you are actively working on creating your baby. Vividly see yourself holding your baby in your arms, smiling, looking into her or his eyes. Feel the happiness. Be a match for the happiness you want to attract, not the upset you wish to transform.

Surrender to where you are right now on this journey and how it makes you feel; resist the need to bury, suppress, run, or hide. You are now actively moving all the roadblocks out of the way and clearing your path. Trust this is happening—because it is.

Acknowledge how you feel every time you hear some else's pregnancy news or see a pregnancy scene in a movie. Each time, follow the same technique until you have nothing but pure joy and happiness flowing through your body, reaffirming to your mind that it is safe to have a baby. Does your heart sink, chest tighten, or stomach knot? Maybe you experience something else. Stop these emotions in their tracks; break the cycle and habit. That's all this is; we are creatures of habit, and habits can be rewired and refueled in a positive way.

Observe your body language when you see the barrage of baby ads on the television or hear them on the radio. If any kind of tensing, tightening, or sinking feeling is occurring, feeding the fear that "it's not happening," change it immediately.

Break down the underlying, untrue notion of "It's never going to happen" or "When will it be my turn?" Take the focus off what you don't want and clarify what you do want to experience.

Delve into any sensation you feel or any image that appears. Each time, you will know what you need to do: cut it away. Is it begging to be freed or loosened? If the image is dark, make it light; if it appears as a ball, kick it over the bar, or pop it.

Even though you may feel the sensation in the same place, the image will appear different each time, as you work through another layer of buried hurt and upset. Notice how the sensation instantly changes as you work with the image.

The more you can change the fine details of the image, the more powerful your healing will be. You will see things more clearly and become more focused. You will feel lighter. You will have more strength, courage, and confidence.

Look closely now; could your situation be easier? Are you clinging, gripping, clawing to the desired outcome? Is it a white-knuckle ride of want, despair, and control?

Are you still saying you're "trying" for a baby? Catch yourself and choose a more inspiring, uplifting phrase instead. Remember, your subconscious mind equates trying with not achieving. Every time you think or use that nonbeneficial expression, your subconscious mind believes the opposite and rejects any efforts of trying. Smile because you are actively working on, creating, and growing your beautiful family.

Implementing these two tips will create a huge shift in the right direction and fast.

You are done trying; all that is left is to achieve. Yay. Find solace in belief and meaning in trust. Release the resistance. Embrace the reality; through this portal of change, you have already learned a tremendous amount about yourself. You are evolving into the amazing parent you desire and deserve to be.

The blessed gift of pregnancy occurs when you are fully open to the possibility and are already in alignment with the joy and happiness it brings. Send out that happiness to receive more of it back because it is the law; it is the law of attraction.

Reclaiming Your Loving Relationship

Wanting a baby so badly can place a huge strain on your relationship; without mindful awareness, things between you both can become detrimental, even driving you apart. This unfulfilled inner want and need often create a wedge between couples, with levels of self-love, self-trust, and self-esteem on the decline and feelings of uselessness and hopelessness on the increase, wreaking havoc with your relationship.

You may have noticed that lovemaking has become a chore, a time of discomfort more so than pleasure. Affection and togetherness are dampened by unspoken blame, anger, guilt, all those frustrating emotions building and festering beneath the surface. They put a strain on not only your physical relationship but also your emotional relationship, with tender loving touch dwindling and fading into the far distance.

You might be experiencing this pressure, even to the point of currently sleeping in separate rooms; not that you intended or wanted to, but one night led to the next, which rolled into a week, weeks rolling into months. Before you knew it, this unintentional and perhaps unspoken pattern formed.

The healing power of touch is something to be cherished.

Let us guide your awareness to your relationship. Be honest with yourself; be honest with your true feelings, and notice any unintentionally developed patterns. Are you currently sleeping in separate rooms? Have you both found separate interests? Does it feel like you are going down separate paths?

That's okay. This nonintentional separation over time is more common than you think. It just became a habit; "It's easier to sleep in the other room; I have to be up early in the morning for work." Before you knew it, months or even years have passed, totally unintentionally. You absolutely love your partner, but all the strain, pressure, and tension just got in the way of true togetherness and your connection with each other.

Not to mention the effects of all the hormones, if you are on an IVF journey. I'll tell you a funny story: When my husband and I went through IVF, I had all these hormones raging through my body. I'm not one for medication, so they really affected me. I don't even know what ridiculous tiny thing set me off, but all I can say is, my husband was outside, cleaning the windows at 11 p.m.; the poor man felt safer outside the house than in it.

You have to laugh; you have to find moments of humor, even in the midst of suffering, precious moments of holding hands, kissing, and cuddling together. Your relationship is too important. Remember, you chose each other, for each other—before you ever decided to have a baby.

Expanding your family can be challenging when you want to bring another child into your life. Maybe it hasn't happened as quickly as your first pregnancy, or a devastating loss has occurred in between conceiving your first and second child. Perhaps your first child has special needs; the added worry and pressure can be so overwhelming.

Maybe you or your partner are sleeping in with one of your children ; another habit: "It's easier so we can all get some sleep." This all has an impact; flip-flopping scenarios play out in your mind. You feel under pressure as it is, not knowing how you are going to cope with another child, yet this inner yearning for another baby is incredibly strong, bringing confusion, worry, and doubt.

Reclaiming the essence of your relationship is vital; get back into the same room and lovingly back into each other's arms.

The power of awareness is often enough to rekindle and reconnect, inviting solutions to be seen and implemented to address and settle the fears.

The love is there; you know you love each other. Perhaps you're not saying it as often, or at all. "He knows I love him. She knows I love her." Date nights become a distant memory. Knowing you are loved and feeling you are loved are two very different things. Feeling loved is so very special. The ebb and flow of giving and receiving love is so powerful in the healing process, standing strong together, and that sense of having each other's backs, feeling as though you are on the same page, walking hand in hand, side by side.

Addressing the elephant in the room can be extremely hard, but it is necessary. Those unintentional habits just seemed to have formed, and before you knew it, months rolled by. This surmountable but hidden issue, unspoken and festering within, has an effect on your health, even to the point of feeling physical pain in your body. You may feel a burden, a heavy weight of not wanting to be touched. Your body feels like it wants to reject and avoid lovemaking. You make excuses such as "I have a headache," "I am too tired," or something else.

Many clients have shared this feeling of a wall inside their womb, where it feels like the sperm are blocked and rejected from entering. Each client thinks it is just them. Please know you are not alone in these confusing feelings. Perhaps you feel embarrassed and ashamed to reveal the honest truth. Be honest with yourself now; what does lovemaking actually feel like for you, as opposed to what you think it is like or what you believe is so, based on experiences of months or years ago?

Deep-rooted emotions of unresolved sadness, hurt, and rejection can form a wedge in any relationship.

Bring your awareness down to your womb right now; see what you see. If there is a strain in your relationship, you will see it as something. Let us work with the wall image that usually surfaces; something entirely different may show up for you, so whatever you see, work with it. How high is the wall? What does it look like? Can you climb over it? Can you knock it down? Can you blast through it in one go, or can you take it down, brick by brick, layer by layer?

Experiment further and confirm that your deep unresolved emotions are impacting your physical and emotional relationship with your partner; this proves the burdensome weight of unspoken or unresolved emotions carries consequences in the physical body.

Jennifer Coady Murphy

Facing a Threatening Miscarriage

There are no words to truly describe the pain when you face a terrifying situation like a threatening miscarriage. You have feelings of despair, churning emotions within, along with outer body sensations or numbness. You hear "Go home on bed rest," caught in the distance between waves of weeping, nausea, terror, and doubt.

You're afraid one wrong move, one wrong bend, or a sudden change of direction could result in your worst nightmare. Fear paralyses and numbs your body, but your mind is far from numb; it is suddenly on overtime, overloaded with ten thousand thoughts flooding in. You flick from one negative thought to the next, jumping from one cruel taunt to the next. You feel one sharp criticism after another or recall hurtful memories of blame, accompanied with their piercing physical effects: "This is happening because I should not have done XYZ [or drank the cup of coffee or glass of wine]."

Each acidic, intense thought embeds in your mind like a false truth, cutting into and etching out the pieces of your shattering heart. Sharp disappointments are tinged with blame: "This is happening because …"

Your mind races to every poor decision or mistake you've ever made in your life. You flip-flop from a racing mind to clawing prayer, filled with fear and remorse. The acute pain of what is potentially happening unravels the mind as those old memories surface. Fleeting images of terror of what you don't want flash before your eyes.

But what if the possibilities are not all that bleak?

What if you had more power in this situation than you realise?

What if you could work with your body and mind to overturn this despair?

It might take some persuasion to replace the harsh doubting words with words of encouragement in your mind. All power comes from within you; you have the power to work through and overturn this despair. Instead of feeling sad and awful, what if you could come

120

at this situation from a different angle? How would that change your experience?

What if this was happening "for you" and not "to you?" What if there was just a fear in the background, wanting your attention? Could you find the courage to look it straight in the eye, just long enough to change the image of what you see?

Know that you can; you can do this. Take my hand as I guide you through a powerful shift of perspective. You can play a far more active role in this situation than perhaps you were led to believe. Let us begin by feeling more balanced and in control. Start with a great big, long, soothing, calming breath in, and give a big, deep sigh all the way out. Repeat until you have connected with a sense of calmness, trust, and belief.

Gently bring your awareness right down to your womb; see what you see. What is the very first image, vision, or impression you see? Notice what is happening in the image. Neither wilfully create nor suppress any visions, images, or impressions. Just allow them to arise. The vision may seem totally random, weird, or strange, and that is okay.

What is happening in the image? Is your baby being taken away? Are she on a desert island you cannot access? Is there a sense of him falling? What is happening? Stay with the scene, and allow your intuition to guide you; what do you need to do to change the scene from terrifying to tranquil?

Imagine bridging the gap of fear or creating a safety net; you have all the tools in the world in your imagination. You can even ask for help. Whatever you need is at your disposal; when you think of it, it will appear. How does your image need to be changed or altered in order to see your baby safe in the vision? Your subconscious mind knows exactly what to do. Trust it.

Vividly change the image in your mind's eye. Create a strong cord of connection; see your baby safe and secure. Feel your connection. Swaddle your baby in a blanket of pure love and acceptance; find the perfect place in your womb for your baby to nestle into. Gently place your baby into this perfect place that you have chosen in your womb; imagine tucking her into a Moses basket or nest.

See your baby nestled in that perfect place, all warm, snug, and cosy. Feel your baby being held, nurtured, loved, and cared for as he grows and develops. Invite a golden white light of protection to envelop your womb. Trust this protecting light will remain in place throughout your pregnancy.

See the progression of your safe, healthy, happy pregnancy play out vividly in your mind's eye. Remember, all power comes from within; your body is either reacting to fear or responding to trust, and you get to choose. You have more power in this situation than you know. Trust and believe in yourself; this is the perfect time for you to be pregnant.

What you are doing right now is choosing to face your fears and overcome them; instead of lying in terror, thinking a tsunami of destruction is coming to ruin your life, you are addressing the underlying fears and actively creating a different outcome.

This possibility is your inner right, and it is available to you. You are stronger than you know; use your deep inner strength. You are actively recreating your pregnancy experience. How does that feel?

Active imagining lets you feel more in control; it addresses yours fears head-on, creating a positive outcome and joyous future.

I have guided many clients through this technique, with varying situations of threatening miscarriage, from "no heartbeat" to hearing that precious sound of their baby's heartbeat for the first time.

From "empty sac" to clients seeing their baby on the screen, nestled safely back into the sac at their next scan.

From "no movement" to witnessing the *boom* of that first kick.

From being in the midst of "early or late pregnancy loss" to completely altering the predicted outcome, to that elated moment of holding your baby lovingly in your arms, looking into your baby's eyes for the first time.

Imagine holding your own baby in your arms. Feel the softness of their delicate skin as you plant sweet kisses on their forehead and gently rub the side of their cheek. Feel the joy, happiness, and elation in your own heart.

Allow your heart to overflow, pouring joy and happiness into every cell of your being. Get the scent of your newborn baby. Listen to their breathing, those wonderful sounds of your baby breathing and sleeping. Look deep into your baby's eyes. Add in as much imagery and sensory elements as possible.

Replay this with even more joy and happiness. Remember, when you are pregnant, you take your baby everywhere with you; your baby feels what you feel. Do you want your baby to feel worry, fear, and tension, or joy, gratitude, and happiness? Babies love to feel and be surrounded by joy, radiance, and happiness. They thrive in a joyous environment.

Please trust this process, even though it may go against what your doctors say. You are stronger than you know. You can do this.

One client phoned, hysterically, after her scan, where she heard was told, "The sac is empty." Distraught and devastated, she came straight in to completely break the onset of trauma setting in.

The guidance came to me to just say, "Aw, you have a fun little one on her way; she wants to play hide-and-seek," which took her by surprise and captured her attention enough to allow the opportunity for her to exhale.

We brought her awareness right down to her womb and guided her to let her subconscious mind find her baby.

"Can you see her?"

"Yes."

"Excellent; well done."

I encouraged her to smile and take some nice, long, deep, calming, soothing breaths, as she connected with her baby by playing hide-and-seek.

Okay. Your turn. Your baby wishes to play hide-and-seek. Are you ready to play with your baby for the next few minutes? Yes? Great, so smile and have fun. As she played hide-and-seek in her imagination, everything changed.

Her confidence grew; her energy, strength, and reassurance were enhanced. She looked her fear directly in the eye and realised it wasn't so scary, after all.

Notice how you are enjoying this experience of playtime. See what you see. Feel how you feel. Hear what you hear. Listen to the sound of your laughter. Listen to the sound of your baby's laughter, loving this connection of playing together.

Enjoy yourself, and give your fear permission to melt away and dissolve completely. Taking all the time you need, give your baby a loving hug. Please thank your baby for playing with you. Swaddle your baby in a blanket of pure, unconditional love and acceptance. Imagine tucking your baby into a Moses basket; place her gently back into the sac. Tuck her in and tell her how much you love her and adore her; you cannot wait to play with her at the end of your safe, healthy, happy pregnancy.

See that strong cord of connection between you and your baby.

Two days later, at the next scan, guess what? It wasn't empty anymore. Her baby was safely nestled back in the sac. All was well throughout the rest of the pregnancy.

In fact, it was better than well; a whole new element of vibrancy and joy took over. The underlying hidden fear for this client was she thought she would not be able to play with her child. She felt jealous and terrified when she saw the playful interactions her friends had with their children. She was not a playful child herself and feared not being able to experience a playful connection with her own child.

In the background, that fear festered and built up to be so insurmountable that it affected the pregnancy. Her body wanted to protect her from those fears, but once the fear was addressed, and she had the opportunity to prove to herself she could indeed play with her child, everything changed.

Another client devastatingly lost their first baby at six days old, due to complications during birth. After a long time, they cautiously became pregnant again. As the pregnancy progressed, she became aware that there was no movement; she could not feel her baby at all. The doctors were alarmed and gave the prognosis that this pregnancy would not continue, resulting in a spontaneous abortion.

After some calming breathwork, we used her imagination and subconscious mind to see her baby. The first image that popped in was her baby on a desert island, drifting away, encircled by sharks. Initially, there was no way of accessing the island. We worked with the image, changing the sharks to dolphins; instead of the island drifting away, we drew it closer and imagined bridging the dread-filled gap of murky waters.

Then all of a sudden, a huge surge of energy coursed forward, along with a great big "boom." The baby kicked so hard, I felt it ricochet through my hands resting on the client's shoulder and knee.

The enchanting intertwining and embracing of their energies was so powerful, it was the most moving, miraculous experience I have ever witnessed. The whole room filled with a powerful vibration of pure loving energy; it was tangible. Tears trickled down my face and overflowed from the client's eyes. During this session, my client connected to her growing baby and also to her first baby, whom she had felt disconnected from; terrified and afraid, she thought her first baby hated them and would think he had been forgotten and replaced.

At that exact moment, the most precious reassuring memory arose. During the numbing devastating loss, at the centre of all the pain, she remembered holding her angel in her arms. Time stood still as she said her last goodbye.

Peace in that moment embraced her, like one of those strong, loving grandmother's hugs you melt into, the kind that musters up the strength to carry on.

Her entire body filled with pure peace, the most sensational peace and strength imaginable; she felt as though she was in heaven herself. That reassuring, peaceful feeling of unconditional love in its purity washed over her once more, and in that moment, she just knew her baby held no grudge; he was filled with only the purest unconditional love that held no bounds.

She trusted that her little angel is a beautiful, guiding, loving light, ever present in her life, that could not and would never be replaced. She felt empowered by the thought that no lifetime could sever the eternal bond they shared. He was a guardian angel, a big brother, bringing immense peace and solace, along with the comforting inner knowing that this birth would go smoothly, which it did.

The remaining duration of her pregnancy was a completely different experience. It was joyous and exciting, filled with movement and kicks. This process allowed them to start the healing process; they felt blessed and grateful to have both of their little men in their lives, just in different ways. Such a heart-warming, moving experience was filled with hope, positivity, trust, and belief.

Exercise to Verify the Effects of Relationship Strain in the Body

❖ Stand beside your partner, and extend your arm straight out.

❖ Bring to mind the image of someone you love and adore, a person or a pet who instantly brings a smile to your face just by thinking of them.

❖ Hold that image in your mind as you hold your arm out.

❖ Ask your partner to press down on your extended arm as you resist against her or him, keeping your arm extended out.

❖ Notice how strong you are. When your partner presses down on your arm, your arm should feel super strong, and he or she should not be able to push your arm down. The psychophysical response, which is the relationship between a stimulus and sensation, is positive and strong when we think of someone we love.

❖ Now think of someone you do not like or trust.

❖ Extend your arm out again, and ask your partner to press down on it.

❖ What happened that time? Your arm felt weaker, and no doubt your partner was able to push your arm down. Right? This time, you psychophysically responded to the negativity and dislike felt for that person, which created a weakness in your system, making your arm drop.

❖ Now think of that first positive person again; just by thinking of them, your strength will return.

Did you know there is a strengthening and weakening effect of hugging?

Hugging to the right, or hugging to the left?
What is the difference?
Heart-to-heart hugs or liver-to-liver hugs?

❖ Heart-to-heart hugs are amazing; they not only strengthen your physical body, your mind, and your soul, but they strengthen the other person and your relationship.

❖ Hugs on the opposite side create a weakness; why? Because the liver is on the other side; it is responsible for eliminating toxicity in the body on all levels, physical, emotional, and mental. Now that your awareness has been drawn to the difference in hugging, you will very clearly feel the difference.

❖ Experience both types of hugs with your partner, and do the arm tests again.

❖ Did the heart-to-heart hug feel strengthening? Did your arm stay up or fall down?

❖ Please note that if your arm fell down with the heart-to-heart hug, you did not do something wrong.

❖ The only reason the heart-to-heart hug with each other did not strengthen you and your arm dropped—even though you both very clearly love each other—is because knowing you are loved and feeling you are loved are two very different things.

If there is unresolved sadness, hurt, or rejection beneath the surface, festering under the skin, tucked away in the subconscious mind, this adds to the feelings of hopelessness and despair of trying for a baby. It may even feel awkward and uncomfortable to hug at all.

Please note that giving each other a heart-to-heart hug each day will melt away the years of accumulation, and it will begin to feel nice. Each and every hug becomes more comfortable, loving, and wonderful. As of today, commit to daily heart-to-heart hugs, and reclaim the togetherness of your relationship.

It is simple to do and simple not to do, but please do not underestimate the power of this simple technique to get your strength, power, self-confidence, and most importantly, your loving relationship back on track.

Let me take you back to seeing and meeting your partner for the first time. Recall to mind the very first time you met.

What did that feel like?

What attracted you to your partner?

When you first dated, what did you do? Where did you go?

Remember, you chose to be with one another before you chose to bring a baby into the world. Take time to rekindle your relationship; bring the spark back by first focusing on what attracted you to them. What gave you those butterflies in your tummy?

Remember how much more self-love, self-trust, and confidence you felt then. Fears, not communicating with your partner, or not expressing exactly how you feel because you do not want to hurt them only builds beneath the surface. I hear "I went along with IVF as I thought that's what you wanted" all the time. The relief when couples are finally on the same page is huge. It is a total game changer; you can see it on their faces, hear it in their voices. Everything comes together in a united way when the elephant in the room has been addressed.

What elephants are in the room for you?

What are you afraid to say? Can you voice how you truly feel with your partner?

Be open and honest. Share it with them, or at least write out your fears on paper and burn it. Move the stuck energy, pain, hurt, and sadness out of your system, out of your mind, and out of your body. It is vital to get this heavy, stagnant stuff out of your body to create the space you need for your beautiful baby.

Reclaim your loving relationship. Remember, your partner chose you; she or he loves you. There was no ultimatum: "I'll love you if you give me a baby." He or she chose you first and foremost. It begins with you, being honest with how you feel right now in your relationship and about your relationship. Accept yourself right now for who you are, as you are. You are important. Accept your partner for who he or she is. He or she is important too. Accept your relationship, meeting it exactly where it is (not where you think it is).

How is your relationship today? What is working well?

What is not working well?

What habits of avoidance have crept in, unbeknownst to you?

What do you need to change to make the partnership more loving and less avoiding?

A loving, happy relationship, standing strong, side-by-side, together, hand-in-hand, must be reconciled now, before bringing your child into the world. Create a happy, inviting, loving, welcoming home.

Dear Caring Parents, Family, and Friends

May I Suggest ...

I am so excited for you. I know you are so eager to have grandchildren to spoil, love, and adore. It will happen; life has many windows and doors of opportunities. There is always a way, but sometimes, underlying emotional issues need to be healed first. Be open to and mindful of honoring the journey your son or daughter is on; give them positive encouragement, listening, as opposed to assuming.

You are coming from a wonderful, loving, supporting place, but unintentional worrying and concerns may be contributing to the accumulation of fears, blocks, and barriers that are already there, resulting in the total adverse effect to your caring support.

I fully appreciate you are worried about your son or daughter becoming a parent, but the worst thing you can do is worry. All worrying does is make you sick; it gives you sleepless nights and irritates your son or daughter.

Why?

Because you worry about the things you do not want to happen; you worry about them being childless, worry about miscarriage, worry about a child with disabilities, worry about difficulties or complications, worry about what the neighbours or family members will say. Whatever the worries are, it is always on the negative side, and if you worry hard enough, as with the law of attraction (what you think about, you bring about), you will end up in an overwhelming situation, feeling, "That is exactly what I didn't want to have happen. That's just what I feared would happen." Then you start beating yourself up and experience more sleepless nights: "I knew that was going to happen; I could see that happening."

Does this sound familiar? Have you ever experienced that?

Before the thinking mind jumps in with "Oh, I'm to blame," please know, there is absolutely no blame here, only learning and growing. Blame serves no purpose, and you were not aware of this before. There is great power in knowing that you can do something really helpful and beneficial for your son or daughter and restore your own sleeping pattern by shifting to a positive perspective, focusing on what you actually wish them to experience in life.

Actively help them on a positive path to experiencing parenthood for themselves. Refocusing your awareness also shifts your strong energy behind your thoughts to emotionally charge the situation in a positive, empowering way for your son or daughter.

As a parent, you would do anything to protect your child; you would go to the end of the earth for your child, no matter how old they are. True? Yes.

Now feel the strength of that protective energy and see how much love you have for your son or daughter. You haves such strength and courage when it comes to protecting your children.

So when you worry about them, know now that there is phenomenal protective strength and energy behind those worries; this will not only make you sick from worrying and give you sleepless nights, it will also take the positive energy away from focusing on exactly what you do want for your son or daughter, as opposed to what you don't want.

How can you change things around?

Energy flows where attention goes.

Instead of worrying about your son or daughter being childless, reroute your powerful energy to visualising them with their own child or family. See it clearly in your mind's eye, without any shadow of doubt. Visualise the excitement, the smile on their face, the joy in their heart, the light in their eyes; hear them say, "Yes, we did it."

Instead of worrying about them miscarrying, visualise them thriving in pregnancy, loving their safe, healthy, happy pregnancy. See clearly that beautiful pregnancy radiance all around them, like a warm glow, excited and happy. Now is the perfect time in their lives to bring a baby into the world; see the couple as great friends, life partners together. Hear them laughing, having fun, and enjoying themselves. See their warm, welcoming house as a loving home to bring their baby into.

Instead of worrying about your son or daughter with the type of partner who is no good for them, visualise them meeting the perfect partner. See them in a loving relationship with a kind, caring person. Look for the good; allow your energy to work with the law of attraction in a positive way, and acknowledge the good when it arrives.

This is the empowering way you can help your child; your child will always be your baby, regardless of how old they become.

Instead of fearing complications and difficulties, sickness, or disabilities, see a safe, healthy, happy pregnancy, an easy birth, a perfectly healthy baby.

Instead of worrying about your son or daughter being unhappy and stuck in life, visualise, sense, and feel their happiness. See them smiling and thriving; hear the sound of their laughter. See your son or daughter coping with any challenge life presents. There is nothing they cannot overcome. Trust that you raised them well and the seeds of your wonderful guidance filtered into their subconscious.

Ignite all your senses; see in full detail your strong energy supporting, helping, and enhancing their desired goal. How different does that feel? See what you see; hear what you hear. What does it feel like to see them achieve their goal? What does it smell and taste like?

Instead of worrying about your adult child who can't get pregnant, visualise them effortlessly becoming pregnant. Visualise them with their own healthy baby, hear the excitement clearly, get that scent of a newborn baby, see yourself hold, kiss, and cuddle your grandchild for the first time.

What is the opposite of what you do not want? Refocus your attention to that, and focus on what you do want.

Energy flows where attention goes.

Shifting the focus of that powerful energy from a negative direction to a positive one will not only attract the desired outcome you wish for your son or daughter, it will also strengthen your own immune system and boost your own health.

Which is better: worrying yourself sick, sleepless nights, the anguish of seeing your child upset, or the pleasure of seeing your child thriving, seeing their wishes come true in life? Share the joy. Feel good and strong in your own body, with a boosted immune system, healthy and vital, the excitement of feeling confident and happy about your son or daughter's future.

You get to choose.

Let's Do Another Exercise

❖ Think of the most prominent worry you have about your son or daughter; think of those prominent worries, and repeat them over and over in your mind.

❖ Now, tune into your body and acknowledge how you feel; notice the precise areas of pain, tightness, and tension in your body.

❖ Tune into those pains, one by one; what does it feel like?

❖ Put an image to it; what does that pain look like? Perhaps it looks like a rope or a concrete block; work with the first image or impression that pops in.

❖ Now what does that image need in order to change it? Can you untie the rope, or does it need to be cut away? Know that you can use all the tools in the world in your imagination; for example, do you need a kango-hammer to break up the concrete? Work with whatever image pops in for you. You can even have help from others; for example, if there was a boulder in the middle of the road, imagine a group of people helping you push it off the cliff. Just change the image however it feels like it needs.

❖ Repeat the worries in your mind. Notice the difference; has the pain or discomfort gone? Yes? Well done; you have just completed a powerful exercise to release stress, tension, worry, and sickness out of your physical body and mind. The pain will definitely have changed, but if anything lingers, just tune into the sensation in your body, and change the image until the pain is gone completely.

❖ Now let's take the exercise a step further. Visualise exactly what you wish for your son or daughter: a loving relationship, a happy healthy pregnancy, an easy birth, a healthy baby.

❖ Replay those visualisations over a few times.

❖ Now tune into your body. How do you feel?

❖ Observe the vast difference; your breath is freer, there's a lightness in your chest and a calmness in your belly, your shoulders, jaw, and knees are relaxed. Feel the brightness, health, and happiness within you.

❖ Stay positive; all will be well. Be filled with trust. Believe in the process of life. Empower your health and well-being by sending your positive, strong, protective energy flowing in a truly supportive way, and watch how your relationship with your son or daughter improves.

Powerful Exercises

Empowering Techniques

Let us recap: You now know when you feel highly anxious or have experienced trauma, loss, devastation. You may feel hopeless, useless, let down. All these negative emotions put your body into fight-or-flight mode, in a state of high alert. Your body wants to keep you safe; your breath shortens. It gets caught in your chest or at your diaphragm, and struggles to move beyond. The little oxygen drawn in by your shortened, anxious breathing circulates predominantly around your internal organs in the upper chest cavity, heart, and lungs to keep you alive.

Not only does your breath shorten by being highly anxious, but you now know that when you are extremely stressed, the first system in your body to shut down is your reproductive system. Yes, you heard right: When your subconscious mind and autonomic nervous system go into protective mode, keeping you safe and alive, your body sees any potential baby as an enemy that it has to block out, keep out, or release because it feels there is too much stress right now. The timing is off. You can barely care for yourself, let alone care for another little person.

The extremities such as your hair and nails will also be affected; they are not as important as keeping you alive. If you notice your hair is dry, nails are brittle, and breath is short of late, then your body is in safety mode; you're not being fully nourished by your breath.

Please know, your body is amazing; it is your number one fan. It is better than your best friend; it totally has your back and is always, always there for you, through thick and thin. On a subconscious level, you have been sending mixed messages. You want a baby, but there are undercurrents of fear flowing in the way. The "What if?" fears call the shots, going against your better judgement and longing.

Maybe this is the first time you've heard this fact and felt it resonate within. That is okay; rest assured, we will work through it, starting with your breathing. Vital task number one, to implement immediately, is getting your body out of protection mode and into a calmer state. The quickest way is through lengthening and smoothening out your breath.

Elongate your breath so your reproductive system can be nourished and feel revitalised, recharged, re-energised, needed, wanted, useful, and important. It does not like to feel neglected, no more than we do, and flourishes with acknowledgement and attention. It must feel safe enough to conceive, to hold and nurture your baby.

Genuine self-care is essential for feeling good, liking yourself, accepting yourself, loving yourself. Take relaxing time out for you to feel comfortable in your own skin, to house and welcome your baby into your body and, ultimately, into the world.

Sooo Hmmm Breathwork

This profound breathwork technique is imperative to reduce stress levels and bring balance and harmony to your body and mind. For most effective results, do a number of cycles first thing in the morning before getting out of bed, last thing at night before going to sleep, and as often throughout the day as you need: before going into a meeting, before making an important phone call, before doing anything that you know triggers stress.

This will help to bring calmness to your autonomic nervous system, relaxation to your body, peace to your mind. It counterbalances your reactions to stress, releases the stress that has already accumulated, and most importantly, breaks down the old habitual structure of built-up stress. Breathwork is extremely powerful, so please do not underestimate its immense benefits.

Sooo Hmmm Breath

Inhale, whispering *Sooo* in your mind.
Exhale, whispering *Hmmm* in your mind.
See those words clearly in your mind, and elongate them.
See all the oooooooos after the Sooo.
See all the mmmmms after the Hmmm.
Continue to breathe, using those powerful words, for six rounds.
Inhaling sooooooooo.
Exhaling hmmmmmmm.
Take the breathwork further, and imagine your breath and those words travelling up and down your body.
Inhaling sooooooooo all the way down to the tips of your toes.
Exhaling hmmmmmm all the way up to the crown of your head.
Take the breathwork even further; imagine your breath and a green light, a vibrant green light travelling up and down your body.
Imagine that this green light is magnetic.
It will gather up all the stress, tension, pain, worry, fear, anger, frustration, and irritation being released from your body.
Inhaling sooooooooo all the way down to the tips of your toes.
Visualise the green light travelling with your breath all the way down to the tips of your toes.
Exhaling hmmmmmm all the way up to the crown of your head.
See the green light travel up to the crown of your head.

Now give yourself permission to release even more stress, tension, pain, worry, fear, anger, frustration, and irritation, be it known or unknown. Sense and feel the muscles and joints opening to release and let go; see the muscles opening, just like a bud opening to flower, and see the stress held within release and fly up to stick to the green light. This green light will travel up and down through your body with your breath, gathering up all the old stresses you have released.

When you feel ready, see everything attached to the green light being recycled into joy and happiness; for example, see the green light and all attached to it turn into a bunch of colourful balloons on strings that you are holding in your hand. Sense and feel your hand opening to let go of the strings. See the big bunch of balloons fly up into the sky, a gentle breeze carrying them away. Follow the balloons as they float away. Notice in the distance a group of children playing. One child spots the balloons and points up; they all look up and smile. See them jump up and down with delight; hear their laughter.

Use whatever visions, images, or impressions that feel right for you to recycle, dump, or transform that stress and tension.

Inhaling sooooooooo all the way down to the tips of your toes.

Exhaling hmmmmmm all the way up to the crown of your head.

Write It Out

When old hurts, bitterness, and resentments are stored and held, if they are not dealt with on the level they need to for healing, they will form into physical growths, inflammatory disorders, and dis-easeful ailments, such as ulcerative colitis, cysts, fibroids. Any disease you may be diagnosed with that has "-itis" on the end indicates that you are storing some kind of anger, rage, resentment, bitterness, frustration, jealousy, or hatred. It could be from recent events, or it could be from decades ago; either way, it needs to be released from your physical body, your mind, and your emotions. The fastest way to do that is to write it out.

❖ Get a pen and some paper, and begin to write a letter.

❖ Address it to whoever hurt you physically, mentally, or emotionally in your life.

❖ Write directly to them. You are not going to give it to them; you won't send it to them. No one will read it, so be brutally honest.

❖ No holding back; write out all the things you wished you could have said, all the things you want to say, all the things you need to say. You may use as much colourful language as you wish. Scream, shout, let it all pour out onto the page.

❖ For example, "This is how I felt when …"

❖ Just keep writing.

❖ Keep writing and writing until you cannot write anymore.

❖ Begin to notice the change, the dawning realisation that you no longer actually feel the way you did.

❖ Notice the golden nugget, the hidden gem of awareness that has also surfaced.

❖ Something else will reveal itself.

❖ Something you did not even know you felt that way about, something you had no idea was impacting you in the background, perhaps something you blocked out. Something that was once meaningful now seems trivial.

❖ Feel the freedom this revelation has on you.

❖ You are truly ready to let that go.

❖ You can feel the instant healing effect of this powerful insight.

❖ Then take that letter and burn it.

❖ Repeat the process, if you need to address other people or situations in your life.

❖ Send loving kindness and loving forgiveness to those you have hurt you in the past. People are coming from the best place they know how, and you are learning to reclaim your power and step forward onto your bright path of endless possibilities. Your past does not define you. Your past no longer impedes you. You are free to choose and create your future.

❖ Smile into that idea.

Rolling a Tennis Ball on the Soles of Your Feet

Did you know that every part of your body is mirrored onto your feet?

Both soles of the feet together are reflective of the whole back.

The right sole is reflective of the right side of the back; the left sole is reflective of the left side of the back.

Now imagine the right side of the back is divided into three sections on the right sole. The first section down along the spine is reflected from beneath the big toe down to the heel, not on the big toe but from the ball of the foot down along the inner arch.

The second section down the middle of the right side of the back is reflected on the centre of the foot, beneath the toes down to the heel. Not on the toes but on the ball of the foot.

The third section along the outer edge under the shoulder down the waist is reflected beneath the baby toe and down the outer edge of the foot.

Now visualise those three sections on the foot.

Let's start first by gently observing the body; notice how your feet feel, how your knees, hips, back, shoulders, neck, and jaw feel.

Then place a hand on the wall for support. Lift the right foot (we are going to work section one first), and place the right foot, starting on the ball of the foot, directly beneath the big toe, onto a tennis ball, firmly yet intensely, and slowly roll in one direction down along the inner arch or instep of the foot. Don't just roll it over and back or up and down.

Consistently roll from beneath the big toe down to the heel.

When you find a hot spot or painful area, it is very important that you hold on to that place and say, "Hello. Thank you, and goodbye."

Why?

Because subconsciously, patterns, structures, and paradigms have been set in place, sending messages to the body, telling it to hold stress and tension, and accumulate it in certain areas. Perhaps for you, it is on the back, the neck, or the jaw, wherever you notice stiffness, tightness, or inflexibility. Our bodies are so good; they do exactly what they are told, on a subconscious level.

The issue here is that people have no clue what messages they send to their body subconsciously, and then, they hate their bodies for following the embedded commands and demands.

With this method, just as with changing an old pattern that no longer serves you well, the old effects of that pattern are held in the physical body and need to be acknowledged, changed, and released. A tennis ball is a fabulous tool for this exercise.

You've probably seen children go over to their mother, especially when the mother is in conversation with someone, and say, "Mom, Mom, Mom, Mom," and when the mother says, "Yes, love," the child just runs off. They did not need anything more than acknowledgment.

These stress hotspots on the feet are the very same; once acknowledged, they will instantly release, creating an immediate effect in your foot and also in the reflecting zone of the body.

Change cannot happen unless what needs to be changed is acknowledged; first say hello. Then express gratitude for the effort; your body thought it was doing a wonderful job holding onto this stress and tension. Say, "Thank you." Follow this by letting go: "Goodbye."

You can even have fun firing the old patterns: "I'm too old," "Time is running out," "I'm too fat," "I can't get pregnant," "I'm not worthy." None of that is true, so say goodbye to the clutter of your mind and body.

Set the intention to experience freedom, flexibility, movement, lightness, brightness, health, happiness, joy, fun, and laughter. Change "I can't get pregnant" to "I can, I will, and I am": "I am loving my healthy, energetic, radiant, happy pregnancy" (or whatever it is you wish to experience in your body and life).

Up to now, there has been so much talk, focus, and attention on pain, loss, symptoms, and blame; with the constant law of attraction, the universe is going to have to give you what you ask for by your focus and attention. Whether you realise it or not, your focus has been backwards. Therefore, you experienced lots of that pain, stiffness, tightness that you focused on. But now, you know different, and going forward, you'll talk about and focus on what you truly wish to experience in life and in your body.

Allow your new conversation to be "I acknowledge the past, but every day in every way, I am feeling lighter, brighter, healthier, and happier." Say, "I am feeling confident and empowered." This is happening. I can, I will, I am.

Hold onto the painful hotspot and say, "Hello, thank you, and goodbye." Invite the new intention to filter in and implement, then move on to the next place.

You are not dwelling on anything here, just acknowledging and moving forward. It is important not to dwell on any memory if it surfaces; please know, should any memory surface, it is only coming up to be released. You are ready to let it go; dwelling only gets you stuck in the past, stuck in pain, past hurts, past loss, and disappointment. There is no need because you are healing and moving forward.

Only look back to see how far you have come, so your subconscious mind can see beyond pain and hurt. It allows the pathway of life to highlight, open, and unfold before you.

See the stepping stones of life: If I did not do that, I would not be doing this today. If I did not let that person go, I would not be with this person today. You begin to see the stepping stones more clearly; everything happens for a reason, for you and not to you, as perhaps you once thought. People come into and out of your life for a reason. Your subconscious mind begins to shift into a new perspective.

Try this new phrase: "I acknowledge the pain, but every day in every way, I am freer, lighter, brighter, healthier, and happier." You are acknowledging the pain, but you are not dwelling on it; you are moving forward in life. Enjoy freedom from past blocks and barriers, feel empowered and ready to attain your goal, and most importantly, connect to and understand your pregnancy journey.

This immense shift, moving and releasing, allows you to be lifted out of pain and release old hurts, loss, and emotional wounds. See how deep and profound this exercise is; certainly not a rolling over and back thing.

Procedure

❖ Gently observe your body.

❖ Work slowly and steadily down along each of the three sections on your foot. Acknowledge all the hotspots along the way. Breath through them; do not hold your breath. Notice how heavy and dense your breath becomes; it is the tension being released, being dislodged by saying hello, thank you, and goodbye. Holding your breath will send the message to your body to keep the tension. Releasing your breath sends the message that it is safe to let go.

❖ When the three sections have been complete, step off the ball.

❖ Now acknowledge how your right foot compares to the left; observe your right knee in comparison to the left. Notice the difference between your hips, back, shoulders, jaw; how do they all feel? Do the sides feel lopsided and out of balance?

❖ Work slowly and steadily down along each of the three sections on your other foot. Acknowledge all the hotspots along the way.

❖ Step off the ball, and observe your body again, acknowledging any and all changes, no matter how small they may appear. Notice them all; are both sides more balanced, open, relaxed, and harmonised now?

❖ Repeat the first foot again; notice the changes from the first time. Is there a change in intensity of the painful hotspots?

Are they less painful, or are they gone? Thank your body for releasing them. Enjoy the new spring in your step. Walk forward with freedom and flexibility towards attaining your goal.

❖ Repeat the second foot again; notice the changes from the first time. Have the intensity of the painful hotspots changed? Are they less painful, or are they gone completely? Thank your body for releasing them. Enjoy your new freedom and flexibility. You cannot beat simplicity in life; a good positive attitude and a tennis ball will give you profound results. Experience it for yourself.

The Secret behind Affirmations

Empowering Positive Attitude Fuelled by Positive Emotion

Just saying the right things, such as "I will get pregnant," is not enough. Can you hear the vagueness in that statement? Can you feel the uncertainty in the energy behind it? You can say positive words and affirmations until the cows come home, but if the underlining feeling in the background is, "OMG, what if it never happens?" that undertone of fear is going to get picked up and reinforced by your low vibration energy, and that is what you will ultimately meet more of on your path.

Please understand, your energy is attached to the feelings of those empty words, which lack trust and belief; it's said for the sake of it because someone told you to say affirmations, or you are trying everything possible.

The fear of your pregnancy not happening will be sent out to the universe, and that is what will get picked up on. That's what you are going to experience more of: things not happening. This keeps you in a state of want, need, and unhappiness, which only attracts more wanting, neediness, and unhappiness. You're stuck on the hamster wheel of same old, same old, feeling powerless, useless, and miserable; all fun, energy, and enjoyment are zapped from the core of your being.

Affirmations are powerful mindset adjusters; when used correctly, they have the power to move you beyond "I can't" to "I can" to "I will" to "I am pregnant," but the secret is, they need to be said with depth, feeling, and meaning, as though you truly believe in your heart and soul that it is happening, and you are worthy to receive your desires.

Set an inspiring intention; the starting point for any successful journey is an energetic vision statement for the future you wish to create, enjoy, and experience.

I am loving my safe, healthy, happy pregnancy, fuelled with radiant health, filled with all the energy and vitality I need to experience this incredible adventure to parenthood and time in my life, with my loved ones supporting me to the fullest.

Create empowering affirmations; they must be positive and in the present tense, as if they are already happening now. Say these positive, present-tense affirmations daily to reconnect with your intention and to help you stay motivated and moving towards achieving your goals. Take inspired action: "I hereby declare to myself and the universe."

- ❖ I am excited and empowered, trusting, believing, and knowing that I have everything I need inside me to fulfil my intention and achieve my desire.
- ❖ I will live my intention and achieve my goal for myself and to inspire those around me.
- ❖ No matter what, I am succeeding. Imagine, believe, and achieve.

Repeat daily with depth, feeling, and meaning. Imagine as if you've already achieved your goal; what does it feel like? Feel that feeling, and really get in touch with it. Feeling that way now will attract more of that feeling into your life. No more waiting; enjoy basking in that feeling now.

Happiness is an inside job; it is not dependent on achieving a goal first. It's the other way around. Be the feeling first, do the inspired trusted action, and have your baby in your arms. Be, do, have.

A strong positive mindset is reinforced by empowering affirmations.

Then stand back, smile, and embrace everything you've ever wished for because it is coming faster that you can imagine. Have you ever heard the expression "Be careful what you wish for"? That applies here because there is no turning back. You are in alignment with your goals and desires; they are coming to you. You will naturally start doing the things you need to in order to achieve your goal. You will soon find you have achieved and have everything you wanted and aimed for.

When there is nothing else to do, all that is left is to achieve and be grateful.

Gratitude

Taking some slow, deep breaths in and out. Invite yourself to connect with the oasis of calm and well of gratitude within you now. Behind closed eyelids, roll the seeing eyes back, and look deep inside. See a peaceful image of serenity clearly in your mind's eye. See what you see, feel how you feel, and hear what you hear. Begin to invite gratitude to flow from your heart into every cell of your being and every facet of your life.

What are you truly thankful for in your life right now? See the images of people, experiences, and opportunities you are grateful for. See all you have positive and joyous in your life flash before you. Aspire now to have more positive and joyous moments to celebrate in your life by fully appreciating what you already have right now;

this is the foundation upon which abundance can flow into and through every aspect of your life.

Allow yourself to be grounded in gratitude. Be grateful for who you are, exactly as you are. Acceptance is key. Silently repeat to yourself, *I love, honour, and accept myself for who I am, as I am.* What is good in your life? What are you truly grateful for? Start with aspects of you. Are you grateful for your five senses: sight, touch, sound, taste, and smell? If you happen to be missing one of those senses, is there a gift in that? Regardless of your situation or what is swirling in your life, there is always something to be grateful for. What is good in your life right now? What else are you grateful for? Your beautiful home, where are you living; do you have a roof over your head and food on the table?

Are you safe? Are you comfortable? Be grateful for your surroundings and the many blessings around you; they need to be acknowledged, nurtured, and savoured.

Think about the people in your life: your partner, your family, your friends, your community, groups that you are involved in, activities that you partake in. Just think of a handful of people you are truly grateful for being in your life right now.

Smile into those thoughts, images, and memories.

What do you appreciate about them? Maybe out of all they do, perhaps there are things that drive you crazy at times, but what can you learn from that? Are they secretly teaching you patience? How do they truly benefit you by being in your life? What do you learn about yourself by being exposed to their personalities and their unique talents? Do you think having more patience would benefit you as a parent?

How about what you currently do for a living? Do you have a job? Are you happy working there? Is there something you do to generate your income that is not serving you? How can you be more thankful for your job, the income you earn and receive? Find and connect to the joy it should bring. Remember, people are coming from the best place they know how, and equally remember, everyone comes into your life for a reason: to help you, to guide you, to teach you to look within.

Who is mirroring something back at you in life, that you can now see clearly, that you can say thank you for?

Acknowledge your own talents, your gifts, your personality. What are the unique, quirky aspects of you that you can embrace? Perhaps not everyone embraces them, but can you embrace them now? What are you thankful for that is uniquely you? What aspects of yourself do you truly love? What skills have you developed, especially since you started this journey? Look back now and tell me all you have learned about yourself since you started wanting to create a baby and bring a new soul into this world?

What talents have you displayed to reinforce the idea of being a wonderful parent? Think about those for a moment; go deep within to connect with a bountiful sense of gratitude. Feel your body relax as you go deep into those feelings of immense gratitude, thankfulness, appreciation, loving kindness, and compassion.

Let those immense feelings of gratitude, thankfulness, and appreciation wash over you; you are truly blessed in this moment. Just breathe it in; embrace its power. Breathe in deep gratitude; breathe out lingering elements of self-doubt, worry, and confusion.

What have you missed that is right there before you? What have you overlooked? In this relaxed state, feel the expansion of your awareness. See things you had not noticed before. Be in a new positive mindset; open your mind to infinite possibilities within you and all around you. Broaden your perspective.

Remember something or someone you haven't thought of for a while who you are also grateful for.

Know that no matter what thoughts may arise when you look in the mirror, you are a beautiful, unique individual. Feel empowered by your uniqueness. No one else like you has ever existed in the world before, nor will they. You are truly unique; embrace and embody that. No one has your unique qualities or individual experiences; no one brings to the table the uniqueness that you do.

147

I encourage you to embrace and accept your beautiful uniqueness in this moment, once and for all. Life has brought you to this point in your life, and this is a wonderful thing.

Gratitude is a choice with your conscious mind, the thinking mind, the intellectual mind; you have the ability to think and to choose. That is a beautiful thing. You have the ability to accept or reject any single thing that comes your way. You do not have to accept any kind of diagnoses or prognoses; you can decide whether to accept it or not. If you reject it, you then have the ability in your mind to re-create and originate your health, well-being, and goals.

You are a creative being; that is a beautiful thing to know. Your subconscious mind operates very differently from the conscious mind; it does not have the ability to accept or reject. It has to accept whatever is given to it; here is the brilliance you can use to your advantage. It cannot determine the difference between that which is real and that which is imagined, which is such an important thing to know, and few people know it.

You get to create your future, not by wishful thinking but by design. Your energy is a vibration that you constantly send out into the world; if your thinking is poor or negative, you will send out a low vibration frequency, focusing on all you cannot do or cannot achieve. That is exactly what you will invite into your reality, more proof to reinforce the notion. But if your thoughts are positive with decisive, committed decisions, a clear vision in your mind, and fueled with positive emotions and feelings of gratitude, you will send out a high frequency, matching and inviting into your life exactly what you wish to experience.

Can you feel the good, can you feel the dawning realisations, the mindset shift you have experienced? Can you sense the good in your life, emanating within you and radiating out from you? You are an amazing person; feel how amazing you are. Your baby chooses you. Your baby trusts you wholeheartedly. Babies don't care if they are born without hair or teeth; they don't care if they are chubby or not, but they care about you. They trust you with every fibre of their being to love and care for them, to nurture them, to guide them through life.

Are you ready?

Yes.

Yes, you are ready. You are worthy to joyously behold and experience parenthood. Breathe it in, and breathe it out, as you remind yourself of the multitude of blessings in your life to be grateful for. Feel the gratitude in your heart; feel your gratitude overflow to every cell of your being. Thank yourself for taking the time to acknowledge all the many blessings you have right now in your life.

Commit to going forth with joy and gratitude in your heart, your beautiful unique smile on your face, and with your head held high.

Love, light, and aloha.

Jenny

Profound Yoga Nidra

It is critically important to strengthen your connection to the subtle wisdom within. Yoga Nidra is a deeply restful practice (it is the equivalent of a full night's deep sleep) that restores your body, mind, and soul.

You will receive exactly what you need from this intricate practice, whether it is rest, intuition, healing, inner guidance, or awareness in a safe environment of the true connection with your inner self. You will build an honest and integral relationship with your body, integrating the vital importance of your cycle.

Maybe you have felt disconnected from your cycle, perhaps even developing a hatred for your period. For some women, for as long as they can remember, their menstrual cycle has felt like a painful curse each month. Maybe you have never been educated on the importance of your cycle, other than being shamed or warned not to get pregnant at a young age. Maybe feelings that you're not good enough have persisted, increasing the pain and discomfort you experience each month.

What is (or was) your relationship with your monthly cycle?

Befriending your period and making peace with it is super important. Once you understand your own unique cycle and its natural ebb and flow, you will be in the best position to care for yourself.

It is important to know and understand your unique cycle in-depth, know and understand your own natural ovulation, become in tune with that unique sensation of your egg being released, connect to that inner knowingness, without a shadow of a doubt. You will know your body's signs and changes, which are completely unique to you. Take back your power from the stress-in-a-box ovulation strips or cellphone apps.

You will then be so in tune with and honoring your natural cycle that your periods will feel different; they will be lighter, less painful; in fact, most people notice the pain goes away completely, and the blood is richer, healthier, and vibrant, which is optimum for a health pregnancy.

I am excited for you to see, feel, and experience the difference for yourself. Say goodbye to painful periods of the past and hello to working with, reading, and understanding your body's natural rhythms and cycles.

Preparing for Pregnancy Yoga Nidra

❖ Lie on your back, stretch your arms overhead, stretch down through your legs, and find a yummy full body stretch. Gently roll your head from side to side, and find a nice comfortable position for your head to rest and nestle into the pillow. Take a few moments to ensure you are completely comfortable so you can really relax and let go for the next little while.

❖ Turn off all disturbances and distractions in your mind, and just invite your eyes to gently close. Take in a big, big breath, then exhale fully all the way out, to let go of the day so far.

❖ Begin by bringing your awareness to your breath. Breathe naturally in through your nose and out through your mouth.

❖ Become aware of your breath and observe it in a whole new way. Feel the cool air gently tickle the tip of your nose on the inhale, and notice the warmer temperature of the exhale.

❖ Begin to gently guide your breath down to the belly. Feel your belly rise with the inhale, and feel your belly lower with the exhale.

❖ Roll your shoulders back and down away from your ears; unclasp your hands.

❖ Create some space and room between your arms and your body.

❖ Relax your fingers and toes. Relax your knees. Level your hips.

❖ Unhinge your jaw, and release your tongue away from the roof of your mouth.

❖ To deepen the breath, add in those powerful words. Inhaling soooo. Exhaling hmmm. Inhale and whisper the word soooo in your mind. Exhale, whispering hmmm. See those words vividly in your mind, and elongate them; draw all the os, as many as you need to reach the soles of your feet. See all the ms rise up to the top of your head.

Know that you are about to practice Yoga Nidra—deep yogic sleep. Your body will fall deeply asleep; your mind will stay alert, following along with the journey.

Know that no matter what sound may resound in the distance, it is unimportant. If a mundane thought pops in, just simply say, "Not now," and bring your awareness back to this journey, back to your breath. Inhaling soooo. Exhaling hmmmm. This is precious time for you.

❖ Now, bring your awareness to your heart centre.

❖ See an arched doorway with double doors to your heart. Reach your hand out, open the door, and step inside. See what you see, feel how you feel, and hear what you hear inside your own heart centre. Neither willfully create nor suppress any visions, images, or impressions. Just allow them to arise.

❖ Now imagine if there were no blocks or barriers. No money worries. Nothing or no one holding you back, not even yourself. What does your heart truly desire?

Know that it is only your job to connect with your heart's true desires; it is not your job to worry about how or when it could happen. So imagine if there were no blocks, no barriers, no money worries, nothing or no one holding you back, not even yourself. What does your heart truly desire?

❖ Begin to set a *sankalpa*, which is a deep-rooted intention, a short positive affirmation in the present tense, as if it is already happening right now, beginning with "I am …"

❖ "I am happy. I am healthy. I am a wonderful, caring mum. I am loving my safe, healthy, happy pregnancy."

❖ Allow your sankalpa to arise, and repeat it three times with depth, feeling, and meaning.

❖ Allow your sankalpa to be planted deep in your psyche and ignite all five senses; what does achieving your desire feel like, sound like, look like, smell like, and taste like?

❖ Feel what you feel; touch your growing baby bump.

❖ See what you see; hold your baby in your arms, and look directly into her loving eyes.

❖ Hear what you hear; hear all the congratulations, coos, and aws.

❖ Can you taste the excitement in your mouth?

❖ Smell the scent of your newborn baby.

❖ See your sankalpa in the palm of your hand, and just like making a wish and blowing out a birthday candle, set it free, free without any grippy attachment to the desired outcome. Set it free to manifest, free to flourish, free to return to you when the timing is right. Trust and believe in the process of life. Trust and believe in yourself. You are worthy to receive.

We are going to do a rotation of consciousness exercises around your body; relax each and every body part mentioned to the deepest level ever experienced.

❖ Now bring your awareness to your right palm, the very centre of your right hand. Feel a warm, calm, relaxed sensation; guide that sensation to your right thumb, index finger, middle finger, ring finger, little finger, back of hand, wrist, lower arm, elbow, upper arm, shoulder, underarm, right waist, hip, thigh, knee, calf, shin, right ankle, top of foot, sole of foot, right big toe, second toe, third toe, fourth toe, fifth toe.

❖ Bring your awareness to the whole right side of your body.

❖ Now bring your awareness to your left palm, the very centre of your left hand. Feel a warm, calm, relaxed sensation; guide that sensation to your thumb, index finger, middle finger, ring finger, little finger, back of hand, wrist, lower arm, elbow, upper arm, shoulder, underarm, left waist, hip, thigh, knee, calf, shin, left ankle, top of foot, sole of foot, left big toe, second toe, third toe, fourth toe, fifth toe.

❖ Bring your awareness to the whole left side of your body.

❖ Bring your awareness to your right shoulder, left shoulder, back of the shoulders, in between both shoulder blades, upper back, mid-back, lower back, right buttock, left buttock; run the awareness along the spine, the whole back together.

- ❖ Run your awareness to the crown of your head, forehead, right eyebrow, left eyebrow, space between the brows, right eyelid, left eyelid, right eye, left eye, and both eyes together.
- ❖ Bring your awareness to your right ear, left ear, inner ears, and both ears together.
- ❖ Bring your awareness to your right cheek, left cheek, and both cheeks together.
- ❖ Bring your awareness to your nose, tip of nose, bridge of the nose, right nostril, left nostril, and the whole nose.
- ❖ Bring your awareness to your upper lip, lower lip, all the tiny muscles in and around the mouth, floor of the mouth, roof of the mouth, gums, teeth, tongue, and the whole mouth together.
- ❖ Bring your awareness to your chin, jaw, and neck.
- ❖ Bring your awareness to the right collarbone, left collarbone, right chest muscles, left chest muscles, whole chest together, abdomen, naval, whole right leg, whole left leg, both legs together, whole right arm, whole left arm, both arms together.
- ❖ Bring your awareness to the entire back of the body, entire front body, the whole body together, your whole body together, relaxing so very deeply.
- ❖ Become aware of your entire body, from head to toes. Observe total physical stillness, calmness, peace.
- ❖ Bring your awareness to the meeting points of the body; sense and feel the gentle touch where the upper eyelids meet the bottom eyelids, the gentle touch of the lips.
- ❖ Become aware of the meeting points between you and the surface beneath, back of your head and surface beneath, your whole back and the surface beneath, the backs of your legs and the surface beneath.
- ❖ Intensify the awareness of your body connecting with the surface beneath you.

Observe your breath, like a silent witness, without interfering with it. Notice the breath flowing in and out naturally, an easy, effortless, relaxing breath. Feel your belly expand with the inhale, and feel how really good it feels to let go on the exhale. Let your body relax further every time you exhale. Imagine your body completely surrendering.

❖ Surrender now; sense and feel a greater connection between you and the surface beneath. Melt into the support that is right there behind you.

❖ Now imagine you are swaddled in a blanket of love, feeling completely safe and secure, swaddled, held, nurtured, and cared for. You're totally accepted for who you are, as you are. Melt into this sensation, and allow any lingering worries to just dissolve away.

❖ Now imagine being cocooned, nurtured, cared for, sinking down, down, down, down, all the way down to the centre of the earth, lovingly held in Mother Earth's arms; draw in all the love and support you need. Receive in as much as you need; release out all you are ready to let go of. Melt into this loving acceptance. You are loved, you are cared for, you are worthy, you are enough.

❖ Become aware of the breath flowing in and out of your nostrils. The natural easy breath flows through both nostrils and meets at the brow centre, forming a triangle.

❖ See your breath as originating outside of you, being drawn in through both nostrils and coming together at the brow centre. See that triangle shape in your mind.

❖ By breathing through your nostrils, you allow yourself to remain in control of your state; when you breathe through your nose, you energise your body's natural bio energy centre. The right nostril is the positive conduit, relating to dynamic energy. The left nostril is the negative conduit, relating to static energy. When the flow of the breath is even through both nostrils, it correlates to equanimity or balance. You can achieve total control of your inner state by maintaining the subtle flow of the breath through your nostrils.

❖ Continue your awareness of the breath at the nostrils. Imagine you are breathing through alternating nostrils, breathing in through the right side, out through the left; in through the left side, out through the right.

❖ Continue alternating the flow of your breath in this pattern: in through the right, out through the left; in through the left, out through the right. This is one round. Continue for three more rounds. Alternate your breath mentally, in your mind.

❖ Then inhale evenly through both nostrils, and exhale all the way out through the mouth. Notice the balancing effects on your mind. Both left and right hemispheres of your brain are perfectly balanced. Notice the clarity that results.

❖ We will now develop an even further state of equanimity by noticing the opposite pairs, beginning with the sensation of heaviness; become aware of the force of gravity and the weight of your body. Your body has become so heavy. Intensify the feeling of heaviness throughout your body.

❖ Now become aware of the lightness, the sensation of lightness throughout. Your whole body feels light as a feather, as if you are floating in space. Light as a feather, the sensation of levitation, effortles sly rising up off the ground. Intensify this feeling of lightness.

❖ Now recollect the experience of pain, any kind of pain you have experienced in your lifetime, physical pain, mental pain, emotional pain, physiological pain, the pain of feeling separate; remember the distinct sensation of pain as clearly as possible. Intensify your recollection as acutely as possible.

❖ Now recall the feeling of pleasure. Any form of pleasure, joy, happiness, or excitement you can remember. Pleasure of the body, emotional elation, mental happiness; recall a time in your life when you experienced exquisite pleasure. Remember the distinct sensation of pleasure as clearly as possible. Intensify your recollection of the feelings of pleasure and happiness as acutely as possible.

❖ Experiences and sensations come and go; nothing is permanent.

❖ Allow yourself to melt into this space of perfect equanimity, beyond the changing outer world of duality.

❖ Now float deep within the very core of your being, where you are perfectly content, safe, and secure. Peace and serenity prevail here in this calming space.

❖ Now see the image of an ocean, the dark blue sea, with endless rolling waves rolling on and on across the surface of the eternal infinite ocean This ocean lies within the inner space of your third eye. The space between your brows, the home of your imagination and intuition; it is the unmanifested, unconscious state of your mind. Your body is now asleep, but your awareness remains alert. The silent witnessing consciousness is within the very core of your being.

❖ Tune into your body and say gently, "Hi, beautiful body; what is it that you need me to know?" Listen to its gentle whispers.

❖ Now bring your awareness to the top of your head; invite a wonderful, warm, relaxing, healing sensation to pour into the crown of your head and flow down through your whole being.

❖ Sense and feel it glowing and flowing through you.

❖ Let go of any lingering tension you are holding within your neck and shoulders.

❖ Continue now to guide this feeling through, down the length of the arms through the elbows, the wrists, letting go of the grippy want and neediness, letting go of the need to control things; feel this wave flow right out through the palms of your hands or out your fingertips.

❖ Imagine in your mind's eye what your body would look like right now if this relaxation had a colour. What colour do you see?

❖ See it flowing through your body, relaxing and healing you; even your bones are relaxing, feeling almost fluid. Continue to guide this feeling down through your back, relaxing every muscle, fibre, and cell of your back. Let go of any backed-up anger or frustration. Even your skin and pores are relaxing now.

❖ Guide it down through your waist and hips; now you can really feel your upper body sinking, sinking like a stone, sinking way down. Down, down, down—all the way down to deep relaxation.

❖ Guide this feeling through the front of your body, through your chest, internal organs, glands; it just flows through the ribcage down into the belly and lower abdominal area. Relax all your muscles, every organ, every gland, and begin to feel any hidden stress, worries, and anxieties just flowing away—all the way away from your body.

❖ Guide this feeling down through your pelvic area. Continue to guide this feeling down through your thighs. Your body feels heavier and heavier or lighter and lighter; whatever you feel is perfectly natural. Observe and connect to these feelings. Strengthen your mind-body connection.

❖ Continue to guide this feeling down your entire legs, down through your knees, to your calves, your ankles, the soles of your feet, tips of your toes; with every exhale, your body relaxes even more and more.

❖ You enjoy this feeling because what you are doing right now is choosing: choosing to turn the whole world off, to go deep within, to experience a greater sense of being in control rather than wanting to control. Being in control is a beautiful, relaxed place of ebb and flow, where miracles happen, where anything and everything is possible. This is the calmest, most relaxed and empowered place you have ever experienced.

❖ Strengthen your mind-body connection; float in this feeling for a few more moments.

❖ Behind closed eyelids, roll your seeing eyes back; look to the space between your brows, the home of your imagination and intuition. Look deep into this space; it may seem dark at first, but invite the light to flood in, and invite all the colours of the rainbow in.

❖ Visualise these images clearly in your mind: seeds planted in the ground, a red rose, a positive pregnancy test, a family of trees in a forest, a vibrant rainbow, a curtain of white orchids hanging in the jungle, a moonlit ocean, watering the plants, a clear path, jumping for joy, a glowing pregnant lady, a clear blue sky. Feel the warmth of the sun on your skin and visualise a gentle safe labour, snow-capped mountains, a flower blossoming. Hear the sound of children laughing. Get the scent of a newborn baby. See a vibrant sunrise, a big open road, a colourful sunset.

❖ Begin to think of a soft, healing colour. Let this colour just flow into your mind. If it changes as we go along, that is okay; just let it happen. You're going to use this colour, this healing energy, this light to wipe away any imbalances in your body. It will strengthen your reproductive system and create balance within your whole body.

❖ Begin to imagine this colour that you have chosen, this healing colour, this light; imagine it now flowing in through the top of your head, gently making its way to your pineal, pituitary, and hypothalamus glands. These glands work to maintain proper hormonal balance in your body.

❖ Imagine them glowing with this healing energy, this colour, this light, healthy and strong, functioning at their highest potential.

❖ Guide this energy, this colour down now into your neck and chest.

❖ Guide this feeling, this energy into your thyroid, parathyroid, and thymus glands, strengthening them, clearing any imbalances.

❖ Imagine them glowing with this vibrant energy, with this colour glowing healthy and strong; see them functioning at their optimum potential.

❖ Now see your adrenal glands, sitting there on your kidneys; fill them with this colour, this energy, this light, soothing them. Imagine them balanced, strong, healthy, and well.

❖ Now see this light flow down into your pancreas; fill your pancreas with this colour, this light, this healing energy.

❖ Now guide this healing colour down into your ovaries; fill your ovaries with this healing colour until you can imagine your eggs bouncing with joy, alive, excited, youthful, bountiful; see them glowing and smiling. Allow this healing energy to flow down into your fallopian tubes healing, dissolving any blockages and filling the uterus. Fill the uterus right up, healing it, strengthening it, supporting it.

❖ Begin to feel your body working, functioning at its highest potential in a balanced, harmonised way. Everything works together in harmony, in peace.

❖ Let the healing energy flow right down into and through your cervix. Stay with this feeling for a moment; enjoy it. You can feel the healing happening.

❖ Visualise, sense, and feel this healing light, this healing colour, flowing through your whole reproductive system, strengthening it, creating such a beautiful sense of balance and flow; just let it flow and circulate.

❖ This healing energy, this light, this colour has powerful intelligence; it knows exactly where to go and what to heal. Trust and believe in this healing energy, this healing light flowing through and around you.

❖ Notice you are even beginning to trust your body, beginning to truly trust and believe in yourself and your capabilities; you suddenly realise your body has powerful intelligence and innate wisdom. Your eggs are eggs for a reason; they are already pre-programmed with the knowledge of how to conceive, how to form a zygote, and how to transform into an embryo. Your womb is a beautiful womb for a reason; it too is already pre-programmed with the knowledge of how to hold, nurture, and care for your growing baby.

❖ See the perfect place in your womb right now for your baby to nestle into, to grow and be nurtured, loved, and adored; the realisation dawns on you that your body just needs to get all this stress out of the way; you just need to trust it to do what it's designed to do naturally.

❖ Can you trust your body's powerful intelligence and innate wisdom?

❖ Now imagine for a moment that you are sitting outside; it is nighttime, you are sitting on a beach, there is a fire pit, a beautiful fire with intriguing dancing flames right there in front of you. You are alone but completely safe and totally at peace. There are millions of stars in the sky, and you can feel the air gently touching your face and playfully tossing your hair. Listen to the sound of the waves from the ocean, hear the ebb and flow, gently rolling in and out. You feel so calm, relaxed, and at ease. Peace prevails all around and within you.

❖ Take in a big, beautiful breath, and exhale fully all the way out. Take another big, nourishing breath and acknowledge.

❖ What is stressing you out about this whole fertility journey? What scares you? Be really honest here with yourself, and ask what makes you dread becoming a parent.

❖ Now imagine pulling out a piece of paper with a list from one of your pockets; you hold it in your hand, and you look at it. It is a list of all your fears, all of your worries around becoming a mother, becoming pregnant, any of the fears and worries that you have—no matter how deeply buried and hidden—all are listed right there in front of you.

❖ Now ask yourself, where did I learn this belief? Is this helping me to get pregnant or hurting my chances? What am I scared will happen if I let go of this thought?

❖ Now I'd like you to take that list, crumple it up, and just throw it in the fire. Let it go; let it go because those fears and those worries do not serve you anymore. You are cautious, you are making good choices, you are taking good care of yourself and your body; the fears and worries do not change anything.

❖ So you watch as the list burns and turns to ash.

❖ Watch as the ash flies away.

❖ Watch as it floats away into the night sky. You feel wonderful; there's a deep sense of relief and a deep release; as you allow yourself to be filled with calm, serenity, and peace, you just savour and enjoy this feeling.

❖ In this state of mind, in this state of body, you are whole. You are in control.

❖ In this state of mind and body, there are no limits; anything and everything is possible.

❖ If you can see it in your mind's eye and feel it in your heart, you can experience it in this lifetime.

❖ Recall to mind your sankalpa and repeat it three more times with depth, feeling, and meaning.

❖ See your sankalpa play out in full detail, as if you were watching it on a big screen at a movie theatre. See what you see, hear what you hear, and feel how you feel. Ignite all your senses, and be a match for the happiness you wish to experience so you can attract more of that happiness into your life.

❖ Bring your awareness back to your breath, noticing how smooth and rhythmical your breathing is now. Notice how peaceful yet strong and vibrant your body feels.

❖ Taking in a big, beautiful breath, you may begin your journey back, back to your body, back to the room, back to where you are lying in the room. Begin to introduce some gentle movement, awakening your fingers and toes, awakening your arms and legs. Stretch up through your arms, stretch down through your legs. Draw your knees into your tummy, and give yourself the most loving hug you've ever had. Silently repeat to yourself, "I love, honor, and accept myself for who I am, as I am."

❖ Gently roll to one side; take a moment here to reflect on all you saw, felt, and heard. Whenever you are ready, gather up your beautiful unique smile, your positive "I can, I will, I am" mindset, all your trust, and rise up with your head held high.

❖ You can repeat after me if you choose, "May I receive the healings and blessings I need and deserve for my greater good. May I be free from inner and outer turmoil. May I have an abundance of health and happiness."

Love, light, and aloha.
Namaste.
Jennifer

Breakthrough Results

Jennifer Coady Murphy is a world renowned Elite Inspirational Coach, Top Fertility Expert and Best-Selling Author. Jennifer's goal is that you, not only become pregnant but that you enjoy every precious moment of being pregnant and loving being the best parent you can be. Living in trust and confidence that you are the parent you actually want to be instead of living in fear of being the parent you don't want to be!

Jennifer coaches' clients from all over the world through her Elite Principles of Prosperity International and Conception to College Mentorship's incorporating Bob's – Thinking into Results program – this is the "manual"! Where you finally understand why you behave as you do and why you don't behave as you want to! Why you've been getting your current results and not the results you want!

This truly is the manual every parent wish they had to understand both themselves and their children on a deeper level. We all need a phenomenal mentor to help, guide, inspire and liberate us from our paradigms to empower us on our own personal journey in life. Do you want an incredible mentor to inspire you to take-action? If you want to learn how to be accountable, dive into the mentorship and do exactly what Jennifer says, your results are inevitable! Regardless of whatever you have experienced in the past!! You have the power to create your future.

To guide you to be the best version of yourself and be the best parent you are capable of being? Reach out for elite mentorship with Jennifer +353 87 4506080.